Directory of Surprise Plays for Winning Football:

How and When to Use Them

Also by the Author:

Coaching the Special Teams: The Winning Edge in Football

How to Get Top Offensive Power from Available Football Talent

Directory of Surprise Plays for Winning Football:

How and When to Use Them

TOM SIMONTON

PARKER PUBLISHING COMPANY, INC.
WEST NYACK, N.Y.

Library of Congress Cataloging in Publication Data

Simonton, Tom
    Directory of suprise plays for winning football.

    Includes index.
    1. Football--Offense. 2. Football coaching.
I. Title.
GV951.8.S54   796.33'22   79-4052
ISBN 0-13-215558-3

Printed in the United States of America

Why You Should Make
Surprise Plays
Part of Your Offense

Only 52 seconds remained on the stadium clock as we battled our arch rival for first place in the league. We had the football on our own 21-yard line with fourth down and a long 26 yards to go for a first down. A running play would have little chance of gaining the necessary first-down yardage and would consume valuable time. The defense was set expecting a pass play. Resorting to our list of surprise plays, we called *Screen Pass, Double Pass to the Right,*

Our quarterback retreated looking to his left, then, at the last second, dropped a screen pass to the halfback on the right side. The defensive secondary, which had been expecting a long pass, came up hard to get in on the tackle that would have ended our hopes for victory. Suddenly, our halfback, still in the backfield, threw a second pass into the waiting arms of our split end who had decoyed his way across field behind the defensive backs. He caught the ball and raced 70 yards before being knocked out-of-bounds at the 9-yard line. An unexpected play, well rehearsed and properly executed, had given us a chance for victory when only seconds before we were facing certain defeat. This true enactment of one of our games is only one example of the value of disconcerting plays.

We once led a weak opponent by a narrow 7-0 margin. With only a few seconds left in the first half, an *End Around Pass* gave us an easy touchdown, increased our lead to 14-0, and broke the morale of our opponent. More recently an opponent almost beat us by faking a punt and running down the sidelines deep into our territory. It was a planned surprise play, and it nearly cost us the game.

Nothing takes the place of sound fundamental offensive football. However, more and more I am convinced that a proper blend of well-prepared surprise plays can be a tremendous addition to any offense. Each year we see a greater number of college and professional teams using surprise plays to break open a tight football game.

This directory offers 45 tried and proven surprise plays. Any of them can be adapted to your style of offense. They can be used on any level of football from the younger leagues to high school, college or professional teams. Opposing coaches will fear the surprise plays you use against them because there is little they can do to prepare their players for them. Simply stated, this directory was written to put surprise plays on *your* play list and give *you* an advantage over your opponent.

But just having a list of unexpected plays isn't enough. They must be used at the right time, against the right defense, and against the right defensive players to be effective. You must plan your strategy carefully. Do not overlook any point in considering when to use a particular play and when not to use it. Each play in this directory is accompanied by points of strategy designed to help you decide when and where to use a certain play.

Part I of this directory deals with how to select your list of surprise plays and how to practice them. Part II describes a number of surprise plays that can be used to attack the interior of your opponent's defense. Part III illustrates plays designed to attack the defensive corners. Part IV describes many ways to challenge your opponent's pass defense and exploit its secondary weaknesses. Part V gives ways to use distracting plays in kicking situations, while Part VI examines ways to use surprise plays from unusual formations that take advantage of poor defensive adjustments.

Since it is impractical to diagram each play in this book from every offensive formation, in each case I have selected a formation best suited for illustrating the play clearly. However, you can easily adapt every play to suit you particular offensive formation. Also, most plays will be diagrammed against a 5-4 or 6-2 defense. Slight blocking adjustments may be necessary, depending on the defensive alignment faced by your offensive team.

Remember that surprise plays, unlike regular offensive plays that have been well scouted, must be defended by players on the field within a few short seconds. There is seldom time for help from the defense's coach on the sidelines. This enables you to use the unusual play to coach against the opposing team's *players*, not their coach, for it is the players on the field who must handle the adjustments to the surprise play. If only one play taken from this directory can be the key to an important victory over a tough opponent, that's reason enough to consider surprise plays for your offense.

Tom Simonton

Contents

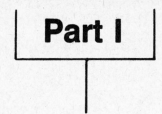

Part I

Planning the Surprise Offense

How to Select and Practice
Your Surprise Plays

Reasons for Developing Surprise Plays

We feel there are at least 12 good reasons why the time spent developing surprise plays is worthwhile:

• Surprise plays provide your players with alternate ways to score if they find themselves trailing and the regular offensive plays are not moving the football against their defensive opponent.

• Surprise plays enable your team to break open a close ball game where neither team can seem to gain an advantage over the other.

• Surprise plays provide your team with a way to build up a comfortable lead in a game where your team is leading by a not-too-safe margin. *Example:* Your team is leading 12-0, but your opponent has been knocking on the scoring door throughout the game. A surprise play could lead to a score that would put the game out of reach for your opponent.

• Surprise plays can take advantage of certain defensive alignments.

• Surprise plays can take advantage of certain weak defensive players.

• Surprise plays can take advantage of overly aggressive defensive players.

● Surprise plays, if used for the first time, have not been scouted by your opponent.

● Surprise plays can demoralize an opponent if your team scores or makes a big gain on the play.

● Surprise plays, once they have been scouted by an opponent, may cause a defensive player to change his regular technique of playing his position.

● Surprise plays cause future opponents to spend valuable practice time preparing for surprise plays that might be used against them.

● Players enjoy practicing surprise plays because of their unusual nature. Putting in a new surprise play is a great morale booster for members of the offensive team.

● Surprise plays are no more difficult to teach and execute than most normal offensive plays.

How Often to Use Surprise Plays

There is no reason why one or more surprise plays can't be used each game as there is certainly a wide variety of surprise plays to choose from. Knowing that your team has them and will use them often will keep some teams from playing their normal aggressive defense.

Some coaches may prefer not to use surprise plays until they are absolutely necessary, while others may want to incorporate one or two into every week's game plan.

One word of caution: Don't overuse surprise plays to the point where players begin to depend on *them* rather than on the normal basic offense.

When to Use Surprise Plays

Timing is very important in determining when to use surprise plays, and of course, this is the responsibility of the head coach. The opening play of the game or the first time your team has the football is an excellent occasion to use one. If successful, it could mean an early score and a quick lead. If unsuccessful, your team is no worse off than if a regular offensive play failed to gain yardage.

Second down and less than two yards to go for a first down is a good situation in which to call a surprise play. The defense would rarely suspect a surprise play in this situation and would probably be looking for a quick-hitting dive play up the middle. Also, if this second down surprise play fails, there is still third down in which to try for the first down.

Use surprise plays with just a few seconds left in the first half. Even if the play fails and your opponent takes possession of the football, they won't have much time left to score.

Even in bad weather, such as rain or light snow, surprise plays can be successful because this will be the time when the defense least expects unusual plays to be attempted.

Using Surprise Plays Against a Weak Team

Surprise plays should never be used to embarrass a weak team. Also, some teams will choose not to show surprise plays that can be saved for tougher opponents. However, we feel there are two times when surprise plays can be useful against a weak team: (1) Early in the game, to gain quick control of the score, and (2) later in the game, if the score is surprisingly close (due to your own fumbles, mistakes and so on).

Using Surprise Plays Against a Superior Team

Surprise plays are most necessary when facing a superior team. Often, a surprise play may be the only way to score against a good defensive team.

When facing a superior team, it is a good idea to have several surprise plays ready. The plays should include a running play, a passing play and a play to use in a kicking situation. Any successful surprise play may go for a touchdown and one touchdown may be all that is needed to upset a superior team.

Although a superior team may appear strong in personnel at every position, you should pick out the most vulnerable area on defense and select surprise plays that strike in that area. One vulnerable area may be at the defensive halfback position where the player tends to come up too quickly once the play develops. If this is the case, use the *Double Pass, Screen Pass* as described in Play 17. If the weakness seems to be a middle guard who is overly aggressive, select Play 1, *Quickie Pass Up the Middle*, or Play 4, *Middle Guard Trap*.

Using Surprise Plays Against a Team of Equal Strength

If is often said that when two football teams of equal strength meet, the team that makes the fewest mistakes will win. We feel that, in many cases, the team that executes the most successful surprise plays can be the winner. Fumbles, penalties, and other mistakes can keep your team from getting ahead on the scoreboard, but surprise plays can overcome that deficit. As when facing a superior team, carefully select surprise plays that will take advantage of your opponent's defensive weaknesses. Keep the surprise plays in mind during the entire game, and look for the most opportune times to use them.

Precautions to Take When Using Surprise Plays

● Don't use surprise plays until they have been thoroughly taught. Nothing looks worse than a poorly prepared surprise play that fails to gain yardage.

● Be sure the defense is set up for the surprise play. For example, don't use the *End-Around Pass* (Play 22) until a regular end-around play has been run and it is certain that the safety men will come up quickly.

● Consider the location of the football before using a surprise play. A *Fake Punt and Run Inside* (Play 28) would be a dangerous play to try inside your own ten-yard line.

● Consider the score of the game. If your team is leading 21-0 late in the game it is foolish to show a surprise play that can be saved for a future opponent. The same idea applies if your team is trailing by a large score late in the game. With only two or three minutes remaining, one surprise play can't make up a 35-point deficit. Also, realize that a tight 7-7 game could be lost by a surprise play which is poorly executed.

● Consider the psychological advantage for your opponent if your surprise play is unsuccessful. A poorly executed surprise play can make your opponent think your team has given up and is resorting to plays which they obviously can't run.

● Don't overuse a particular surprise play. Once a surprise play has been shown, it has been scouted.

● Be sure to warn the officials *before* the game to watch for the surprise play. This can be very important, especially if an unusual formation (see Part VI) is to be used. Make sure the officials understand the formation you plan to use and exactly how the play will develop. It would be disastrous for an official to call a penalty on a well-executed surprise play simply because he was fooled (as we hope the defensive team will be) by the formation used or the execution of the play.

● Try not to alert the defensive team that a surprise play may be coming by inserting a key player into an unusual position. *Examples*: Placing a quarterback at a halfback position may indicate that the offensive team plans to try the *Quick Pitch Pass* (Play 24), or placing the best running back at the punting position can tip the defense to watch for the *Fake Punt and Run Inside* (Play 28).

Practicing the Surprise Plays

All players enjoy practicing surprise plays. The extra ball handling, reverses, double passes, and so on that are often used in surprise plays are sometimes more fun to practice than regular offensive plays. We have found it a good idea to practice surprise plays near the end of practice as a change of pace from regular work. They can give a boost in morale to a tired squad at the end of a long day.

We follow this pattern in teaching surprise plays:

1. Explain the surprise play thoroughly. Diagram it on a

blackboard so that the entire team can see the overall pic-
ture of what the play will look like.

2. *Walk* the players through the surprise play on the field.
Let them step through their blocking assignments and talk
to them about alternate blocking plans they may have to
use against certain defenses.

3. Jog through the play at half speed, getting the feel of
executing it.

4. Run through the play at full speed, working on getting the
timing of the play perfect.

Remember that surprise plays *must* be practiced often, just
like all regular plays. Don't expect to be able to put in a new
surprise play one day and have the players execute it perfectly in a
game the next day.

Part II

Attacking the Defensive Interior

Play 1

Quickie Pass Up the Middle

Basic Strategy:

The basic strategy of the *Quickie Pass Up the Middle* is to take advantage of a hard-charging, aggressive middle guard by letting him come across the line of scrimmage untouched, then cutting him down with a block from the right halfback. The quarterback tosses a short pass behind the middle guard into the open middle area of the defense.

Play Diagram:

The *Quickie Pass Up the Middle* is shown in Figure 1-1.

When to Use It:

● This play works best when used against a team that plays a five-man front.

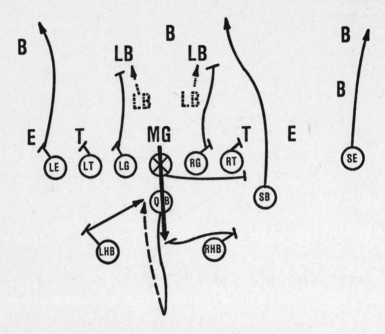

Figure 1-1 *Quickie Pass Up the Middle*

• The middle guard is the key to this play. The harder the middle guard fires across the line, the more successful the play will be.

• The play will develop into a long-gainer if the defensive inside linebackers are reacting quickly to their pass-defense zones.

• The play can be used anywhere on the field, from deep in your own territory to near the opponent's goal line.

• Use this play as the opening play from scrimmage at the beginning of the game, provided you are reasonably sure that the opposing team will be in a five-man front. The middle guard should be particularly aggressive and anxious to get into the offensive backfield, and this is exactly what you want from him to make the play work.

• Since the pass is very short, there is little chance of an interception, thereby allowing the offense to use the play at any time during the game.

When Not to Use It:

● This play will have little chance of success against a five-man front defense where the middle guard plays "soft" (does not penetrate across the line of scrimmage). A soft-playing middle guard will either knock down the pass or tackle the receiver as soon as he catches the ball.

● Do not use this play when the defense has placed seven, eight, nine, or more defensive players directly on the line of scrimmage with the intent of having them all penetrate. *Example*: A tight gap-8 defense involves too many people in the area where the receiver must catch the football.

Position Assignments:

Quickie Pass Up the Middle versus 5-4 Defense

LE—Bump defensive end; take safety man deep.

LT—Block defensive tackle to the outside.

LG—Show pass-block; block inside linebacker your side.

C—Release behind line of scrimmage; block first man to show (preferably the defensive end) on the right side.

RG—Show pass-block; block inside linebacker your side.

RT—Block defensive tackle to the outside.

Split End—Release downfield; take safety man deep.

Slotback—Release down middle of field; take safety man deep.

RHB—Fake pass-block; block middle guard as he comes across line of scrimmage.

LHB—Fake pass-block; turn back to inside, catching pass at about the spot where quarterback takes snap from center.

QB—Drop back 6-8 yards as necessary; pass over the blocked middle guard to the left halfback.

Coaching Points:

Guards—On the snap of the ball, both guards assume their dropback pass-blocking positions. They each count "1,001 . . . 1,002" and then fire out after the inside linebackers who have moved to their pass-defense positions. These guards actually become the lead blockers for the ball carrier. Figure 1-2 shows a drill to develop the guards' technique. Place the two guards a normal distance apart. Station two inside linebackers in their normal positions. On command, the guards pass block for two counts then drive downfield towards the linebackers and block them. A quarterback and left halfback (pass receiver) can be added for more realism.

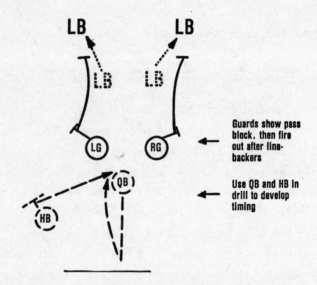

Guards show pass block, then fire out after line-backers

Use QB and HB in drill to develop timing

Figure 1-2 *Drill for guards blocking linebackers*

Center—Make sure the center does not get in the way of the right guard or the right halfback as he moves to block to the right.

Right Halfback—This man is the key to the success of this play. On the snap, he is to open to the right taking his pass-blocking position. As the middle guard crosses the line of scrimmage the right halfback steps toward him, driving his head and shoulder in front of the middle guard, hitting him about knee level and knocking him off his feet. Since the middle guard will not be looking for this block he is usually a vulnerable target. It is very important that the middle guard be knocked down so that he will have no chance to interfere with the pass.

Left Halfback—On the snap, the left halfback sets up as if to pass-block to the left. He counts "1001 . . . 1002," then releases over the middle looking for the pass from the quarterback. The pass should *not* be caught past the line of scrimmage, but on the *offensive side* of the line of scrimmage. Timing is very important and the halfback's timing must be coordinated with the timing of the guards. Use the drill shown in Figure 1-2 to work on the timing.

Quarterback—On the snap, the quarterback drops straight back as quickly as possible and looks for the middle guard's charge. He throws the pass just after the right halfback makes his block on the middle guard. If the middle guard plays soft, the quarterback stays in the pocket and looks for an open deep receiver.

Play 2

Screen Pass Up the Middle

Basic Strategy:

The *Screen Pass Up the Middle* is designed to create the illusion that a downfield pass is to be thrown. As the defensive linemen break away from their blocks and put pressure on the quarterback, the quarterback tosses the football to a back who has stepped into the area between the onrushing defensive linemen and his own offensive linemen. The defensive linemen are no longer in position to make the tackle and the ball carrier has a host of offensive blockers in front of him. The only possible defenders who can tackle him are the safety men, who have been taken deep downfield by other receivers running deep routes, and the linebackers, who should be blocked by the offensive linemen.

Play Diagram:

Figure 2-1 shows the *Screen Pass Up the Middle*.

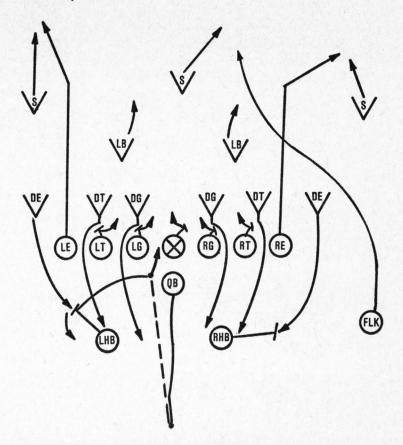

Figure 2-1 *Screen Pass Up the Middle vs. 6-2 Defense*

When to Use It:

● Use this play when the defensive linemen are continually putting heavy pressure on the quarterback as he drops back to pass.

● Call this play when the offensive team is not having success with the long passing game.

● This is a good play to use when a running back is available who can both catch the short pass and do a good job of following his blocking and running in open field.

● Use this play when weather conditions such as heavy rain or snow make the long passing game difficult.

● This play works well against almost any defense. In fact, the more defensive linemen rush the quarterback, the better the chance for a long gain after the pass is caught, because there will be fewer defenders on the defensive line of scrimmage who can make the tackle (see Figure 2-2).

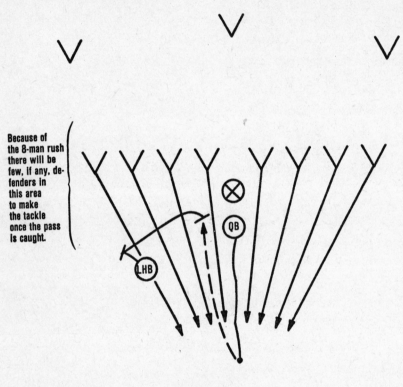

Because of the 8-man rush there will be few, if any, defenders in this area to make the tackle once the pass is caught.

Figure 2-2

● This is a good play to use against a team that has a very strong defensive secondary. If passes can't be completed downfield, complete them on your side of the line of scrimmage where there are no secondary defenders, and then let the ball carrier run for yardage.

● Call this play when the football is located anywhere on the playing field. Since the pass is a short one, there is slight chance of interception.

● Call this play at any time during the game. It is an excellent call late in the game when your team is trailing by a few points. The defense will likely be in some type of deep prevent defense. Complete this screen pass up the middle and let the back run to daylight behind his big offensive linemen.

• Use this play when the quarterback cannot physically throw the football very far. This could be due to an injury to the arm, hand or fingers, or there may be a substitute quarterback in the game who does not have the arm to throw deep.

• Use this play in long-yardage situations such as second down and 18 yards to go.

When Not to Use It:

• This play is not a good selection if the middle guard or any other interior defensive lineman plays "soft" and does not aggressively penetrate across the line of scrimmage towards the quarterback.

• Consider not using this play on extremely short yardage situations *if* the secondary defenders are crowded up near the line of scrimmage. This creates an 11-man front and the play will be difficult to execute.

• The possibility of executing this play successfully declines as the number of defensive safety men and linebackers used increases. *Example*: A defense featuring four rushing linemen, four linebackers and three safety men is a greater threat to stop this play than a defense with six rushing linemen, two linebackers, and three safety men.

Position Assignments:

Screen Pass Up the Middle versus 6-2 Defense

LE—Release; take safety man your side deep.

LT—Block defensive tackle to outside for two counts; allow him to slip by block and charge the quarterback.

LG—Block defensive guard to outside for two counts; allow him to slip by block and charge the quarterback.

C—Set up in pass-blocking position. If a linebacker fires, block him two counts; allow him to slip by block and charge the quarterback.

RG—Block defensive guard to outside for two counts; allow him to slip by block and charge the quarterback.

RT—Block defensive tackle to outside for two counts; allow him to slip by block and charge the quarterback.

RE—Release; take safety man your side deep.

Flanker—Release; take middle safety man deep.

RHB—Block defensive end on your side; stay with him, blocking him to the outside away from the area where the pass will be caught.

LHB—Pass block the defensive end on your side, staying with him two counts; release over the middle (on the offensive side of the line of scrimmage) for the pass from the quarterback.

QB—Take snap from center; drop back to normal passing depth of 7-8 yards. As defenders rush in, drop back several more steps, drawing the defenders deeper into the backfield. Toss a pass to the left halfback over the heads of the onrushing defensive linemen.

Coaching Points:

Ends and Flanker—It is very important that the ends and flanker run hard downfield, trying to draw the attention of the safety men and make them run with them. This takes the safety men away from the area of the pass and gives the pass receiver more room to run once he has caught the ball. Once the pass has been caught the ends and flanker immediately become downfield blockers, working against the safety men who were covering them.

Tackles, Guards, and Center—Once these men have allowed the defenders they were blocking to slip by, they do not release downfield until the back has caught the pass. They face the defensive side of the line of scrimmage looking for a defender to block once they start downfield. They must listen for the back to holler "Go" then lead the back downfield. Two points that must be stressed to these linemen in coaching this play are: (1) Linemen must all hold their blocks on the line of scrimmage for the same length of time before releasing the defensive players. If this isn't done one defender might be putting pressure on the quarterback while another is still being blocked on the line of scrimmage. (2) Once the offensive line blockers have started downfield, *never* pass up blocking the first defender to threaten the ball carrier. It is a cardinal sin to allow one defender to slip through several linemen and make the tackle.

Left Halfback—The left halfback must be sure to make a good block on the defensive end before releasing for the pass. Failure to do this will allow the defensive end to put pressure on the quarterback too quickly and not allow the quarterback time to get the pass off. Once the left halfback has released over the middle for the pass, he should look for any defender left in the area who could stop the play. If no defender is there, he should raise his hands high, indicating to the quarterback that it is clear to throw the ball. Once he has caught the ball, he hollers "Go" to the offensive linemen.

Quarterback—The quarterback always drops back quickly, staying a comfortable three or four yards away from the onrushing linemen. He should watch for the left halfback breaking across the middle. Once the left halfback raises his hands high, the quarterback throws the football. If a defensive player has stayed in the area where the pass is to be thrown, he must be prepared to throw the ball away rather than take a loss of yardage.

Play 3

Inside Reverse
(Wingback, Slotback,
or Tight End)

Basic Strategy:

Misdirection is the key to all three of the inside reverse plays described here. Most defensive players are selected because of their ability to react quickly. The inside reverse plays are designed to take advantage of their quick reactions. All three plays which we will illustrate start with rapid movement by three of the backs in the direction away from the final point of attack. This is done to get the defensive players, especially the linebackers, moving in the false direction of the play. This serves two purposes: (1) It moves several players, probably linebackers, farther from the hole where the ball carrier will hit. (2) It helps set up more desirable blocking angles for several offensive players. All three of the plays offered here can be used with a choice of two blocking plans, trap blocking and straight-ahead blocking. We feel it is a good idea to have all three of the inside reverse plays available for use. This eliminates the possibility of the defense keying on one of the three possible ball carriers. *Example*: If the slotback reverse has been shown in a previous game, have the wingback or tight end reverse ready for the next game.

Play Diagrams:

Figure 3-1 shows the *Inside Reverse to the Slotback* with a trap block by the guard (versus a 5-4 defense).

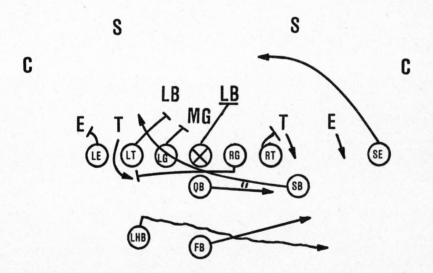

Figure 3-1   *Inside Reverse to Slotback vs. 5-4 Defense*

Figure 3-2 illustrates the *Inside Reverse to the Wingback* against a 6-2 defense using a trap block by the tackle.

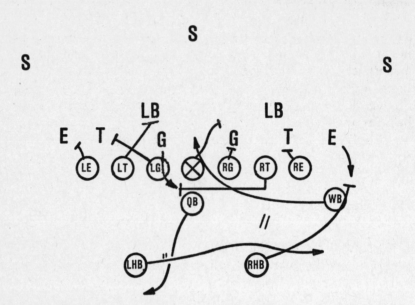

Figure 3-2 *Inside Reverse to Wingback vs. 6-2 Defense*

Figure 3-3 is the *Inside Reverse to the Tight End* using straight ahead blocking against a 5-4 defense.

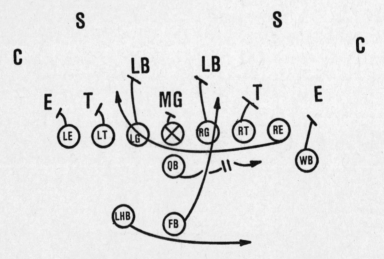

Figure 3-3 *Inside Reverse vs. 5-4 Defense*

When to Use It:

• Use one of these plays when the scouting report indicates that some defensive players, especially linebackers, react quickly to the first movement of the offense.

• Use these plays when the defense begins stopping the off-tackle and wide plays by coming up quickly and plays are needed that hit suddenly back to the opposite side of the center.

• These plays can be used when the defense seems to ignore the slotback, wingback, or tight end as potential ball carriers.

• Use these plays anywhere on the field. They will seldom lose big yardage and can be run with a minimum of ball handling.

• These plays can be run against almost any defense. Be sure to adjust blocking to suit the defensive alignment.

• Use these plays if the slotback, wingback, or tight end is a good open field runner.

• These plays are good selections for long yardage situations.

When Not to Use It:

• The inside reverse plays probably should not be used on the first offensive play of the game. The inside reverse needs to be set up by first running an off-tackle or wide play away from the area where the reverse will later be run. In other words, get the defense looking for the off-tackle or wide play to one side before hitting back to the other side with the reverse.

• On extremely short yardage situations the defense may crowd 11 men close to the line of scrimmage, making the inside reverse difficult to run.

Position Assignments:

Slotback Reverse versus 5-4 Defense (Fig. 3-1)

LE—Turn out on defensive end.

LT—Block inside linebacker.

LG—Block middle guard with center (double-team).

C—Block middle guard with left guard (double-team).

RG—Pull and trap tackle.

RT—Block linebacker.

Split End—Cut across field and block downfield.

LHB—Go in motion to right, attracting attention of defense in that direction.

FB—Sprint to right as if to take option pitch.

QB—Take snap and sprint towards the slotback; give him the football as he goes inside of you (nearest the line of scrimmage).

SB—Follow the trapping guard through the hole after taking handoff from the quarterback.

Wingback Reverse versus 6-2 Defense (Fig. 3-2)

LE—Turn out on defensive end.

LT—Block inside linebacker on your side.

LG—Cross behind offensive left tackle and block defensive tackle.

C—Cut off weakside linebacker.

RG—Block guard.

RT—Pull and trap defensive guard.

RE—Step inside and seal off defensive tackle.

RHB—Block defensive end to cut off his pursuit.

QB—Open to the left and hand football to left halfback.

LHB—Take handoff from quarterback and give football to wingback who is coming to your inside.

WB—Open with left foot and look for left halfback coming towards you with the football. Take ball and follow trap block of right tackle.

Tight End Reverse versus 5-4 Defense (Fig. 3-3)

LE—Turn out on defensive end.

LT—Block tackle to outside.

LG—Block linebacker.

C—Block middle guard.

RG—Block linebacker.

RT—Block tackle.

RE—Open with left foot, take handoff from QB.

WB—Block end to keep him from trailing play.

QB—Fake to fullback and hand ball to tight end.

LHB—Fake to the right side as if looking for pitch.

FB—Fake taking handoff from quarterback and help block linebacker.

Coaching Points:

● All backs not carrying the football must continue executing their fakes to draw the attention of the defense away from the ball carrier.

● Make sure the tight end is well coached on how to take a handoff and hold the football when running. Although backs are drilled daily on this, coaches sometimes forget that ends aren't, so give the end plenty of practice on ball handling before running the inside reverse with the tight end.

● If the tackle trap is used (see Figure 3-2), be sure to drill the tackles on trapping fundamentals. Allow them to work with the guards (who are the normal trap blockers) during trapping drills.

Play 4

Middle Guard Trap

Basic Strategy:

When a team uses the 5-4 defense, the tackles are well coached on how to stop the trap play. They are taught to close down and look inside for the pulling guards who are attempting to trap them. The middle guard is rarely given any instruction on how to keep from being trapped. *The Middle Guard Trap* is designed to take advantage of this lack of instruction.

The middle guard is not blocked initially on the line of scrimmage. Instead, he is allowed to come across the line untouched where he will then be trapped by the wingback. This play can go a long way towards slowing down an aggressive middle guard who likes to fire into the offensive backfield.

Play Diagram:

The *Middle Guard Trap* play is diagrammed using a wingback as the trap blocker (See Figure 4-1). However, a slotback can do the job equally as well if this formation is preferred.

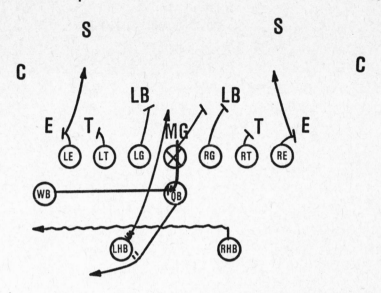

Figure 4-1 *Middle Guard Trap vs. 5-4 Defense*

When to Use It:

● Use this play against a team that plays a five-man front defense with a middle guard head-on or slightly to the right or left of the center.

● Use this play early in the game, perhaps even as the opening offensive play of the game. It will let the middle guard know that you realize he likes to come hard across the line of scrimmage and that you have a plan to slow him down.

● This play can be used anywhere on the field because of the safe ball handling involved.

● Bad weather conditions will seldom affect the execution of this play.

● This play can be used often and not saved for a special occasion. If the defensive team is concerned about the middle guard trap play it may instruct its middle guard to play soft rather than come hard across the line of scrimmage. When this happens you have accomplished your aim—to keep the middle guard out of your backfield—without having to run the trap play.

● This play can be effective during passing downs because the middle guard will normally be planning to get across the line of scrimmage quickly and sack the quarterback before he can pass.

When Not to Use It:

● This play cannot be used unless the defense is in an alignment where a defender is over or very near the center position.

● Do not use this play if the middle guard plays soft rather than coming hard across the line.

● Unless the wingback (or slotback) has been drilled on trapping fundamentals the play is likely to fail.

Position Assignments:

Middle Guard Trap versus 5-4 Defense

LE—Bump defensive end; release downfield.

LT—Block tackle to outside.

LG—Block linebacker over you.

C—Double-team linebacker with right guard. (*Note*: Center could double-team with left guard if his linebacker proves to be tougher.)

RG—Block linebacker over you with double-team help from center.

RT—Block tackle to the outside.

RE—Bump end; release downfield.

RHB—Go in motion to the left; swing downfield to block.

WB—Come hard down line of scrimmage; trap middle guard.

QB—Take snap; sprint behind left halfback handing the football to him. Continue faking around end as if running a quarterback keeper play.

LHB—After the snap, remain in your position (be in two-point stance). Wait until quarterback brings football to you, then cut inside wingback's trap block.

Coaching Points:

There are two positions which need special attention:

Wingback—He must be taught to come very hard down the line of scrimmage looking for the middle guard. He must block the middle guard with the right shoulder (if coming from the left side). Unless this is done, the middle guard could slide off the block back to the inside and make the tackle. The wingback should be drilled on his blocking techniques by working him with the pulling and trapping guards daily. The wingback may need to cheat to the inside a little on this play to coordinate his timing with the backfield personnel.

Left Halfback—If you prefer, the left halfback can take a counter step to the left before taking the handoff from the quarterback. However, this takes a little more split-second timing between the wingback, quarterback, and left halfback than the method listed in the *Position Assignments* section.

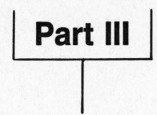

Part III

Utilizing Surprise Plays
Against the
Defensive Corners

Play 5

End Around

Basic Strategy:

The *End Around* is one of football's oldest plays. It has probably been run more different ways and from more different formations than any other surprise play. It is often difficult for the defense to recognize the *End Around* until it is too late. This play combines deception with sound blocking and can be a long-gainer if executed properly.

The play is designed to take advantage of the defensive end. If the defensive end chooses to come across the line of scrimmage hard and tight, the ball carrier (offensive end) can run around him. If the defensive end plays soft and does not commit across the line of scrimmage, the ball carrier will run inside him. There is good faking action by four backs, which will divert the attention of the linebackers and safety men from the *End Around* play.

49

Play Diagram:

Figure 5-1 illustrates the best way we have found to run the *End Around* play.

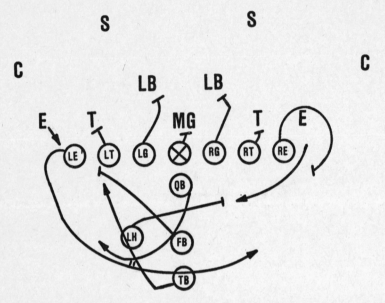

Figure 5-1   *End Around vs. 5-4 Defense*

When to Use It:

● This play can be used whether the defensive end prefers to come hard or play soft.

● Use this play after a good off-tackle or wide play has been run and it is noticed that the linebackers and safety men react quickly to the play, leaving their zones of coverage vacant.

● This play can be executed against any defensive alignment.

● Bad weather will not affect this play because there is no more ball handling on this play than there is on any other play involving a handoff.

● Use this play if the defensive end does not penetrate across the line of scrimmage but instead takes an angle of pursuit towards the other side of the field, leaving his defensive end position un-guarded.

● Use this play if an offensive end is available who can run fast and is a good open-field runner.

When Not to Use It:

● This play should not be used until it has been set up by first running the off-tackle or wide play to the opposite side of the line.

● If the offensive end is primarily a blocker, with no running ability, the play has little chance to gain ground.

● As a rule, we prefer not to use this play inside our own five-yard line. The ball carrier, because of the route he must take immediately after receiving the handoff, will be forced to run inside your own end zone. If he is tackled there it will be a two-point safety for your opponent.

Position Assignments:

End Around versus 5-4 Defense

LE—Open to the outside; take handoff from quarterback and follow blocks by left halfback and right end.

LT—Block tackle to the outside.

LG—Block linebacker your side.

C—Block middle guard.

RG—Block linebacker your side.

RT—Reach-block the tackle.

RE—Release inside defensive end; loop behind him, being ready to block him if left halfback doesn't.

LHB—Step forward with left foot, then turn towards defensive end, blocking him to inside or outside (see *Coaching Points*).

FB—Block defensive end on left side.

TB—Lead-step with left foot; drive into the off-tackle hole as if carrying the ball.

QB—Reverse pivot; fake handoff to tailback; hand football to the end. Continue fake keeper play to the left side.

Coaching Points:

Left End—The left end must make sure his stance is normal when on the line of scrimmage. He must not lean back in his stance as this will indicate he does not intend to fire out hard as if to block. This can be a real tip to the defense that the *End Around* play is coming. Once he has taken the handoff, he should look for the block of the left halfback. If the left halfback blocks the defensive end to the inside, the left end should run wider (around the block). If the left halfback blocks the defensive end to the outside, he must be prepared to run inside the block (see Figures 5-2a & b).

Left Halfback—The left halfback should be sure to take one step forward with the left foot before sprinting towards the defensive end. This avoids a collision with the other backs since they will be moving in the opposite direction. Once he has found the defensive end, he should note his position. If the defensive end is coming tight and hard down the line of scrimmage, he must move towards him and block him to the inside using his left shoulder. If the defensive end is playing soft or loose, the left halfback must block him to the outside, leading with his right shoulder. Figures 5-2a & b show how the block and the running path of the ball-carrying end should be coordinated.

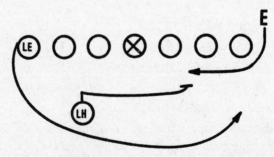

Figure 5-2a *Defensive end comes hard, so left halfback blocks him to the inside and ball carrier runs to the outside.*

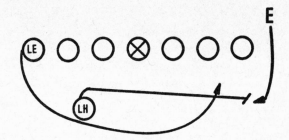

Figure 5-2b *Defensive end plays soft, so left halfback blocks him to the outside and ball carrier runs to the inside.*

Right End—After releasing inside, the defensive end turns back to the inside, watching the play develop. If the left halfback fails to execute his block on the defensive end, the right end should be prepared to block the defensive end as shown in Figure 5-3. If the left halfback makes a successful block on the defensive end, the right end turns upfield and blocks the first defensive player who threatens the ball carrier.

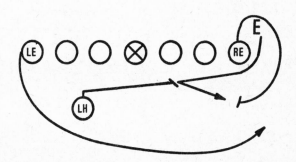

Figure 5-3 *Right end blocks defensive end if left halfback fails to block him successfully.*

Quarterback—The quarterback has two main jobs: (1) He must make a good fake to the tailback. This sets up the play by drawing the defensive players to the off-tackle area. (2) He must be careful not to make the handoff to the end too deep in the backfield. This will force him to run several extra steps before turning upfield. The ball should be handed to the end no deeper than about five yards from the line of scrimmage. The quarterback must carry out his fake to the off-tackle side and never stop to watch the run by the ball carrier.

Fullback and Tailback—The fakes of the fullback and tailback into the off-tackle hole will determine the success of this play. Both the fullback and the tailback must drive into the off-tackle area with the fullback blocking the defensive end and the tailback carrying out his fake even after he crosses the line of scrimmage.

Fake Sweep, Slotback (or Wingback) Reverse

Basic Strategy:

All teams have some type of sweep play. For many teams it is their "bread and butter" play and features one or two pulling guards. Most defensive players know that to stop an offense they must be able to stop the sweep play, and therefore, they are taught to react quickly once they see the sweep play start. Because of this quick reaction to the sweep play, the *Slotback Reverse* has an excellent chance to succeed. The play is similar to the *End Around* play, as it depends on misdirection to eliminate several would-be tacklers.

Play Diagram:

Figure 6-1 shows the *Slotback Reverse* against the 5-4 defense. With slight adjustments, this play can be run using a wingback if this style of offense is preferred.

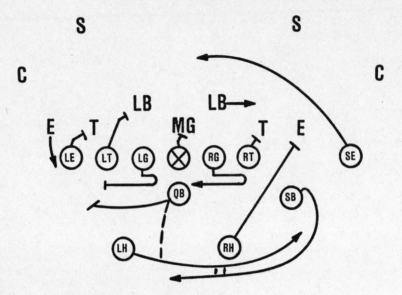

Figure 6-1 *Fake Sweep, Slotback Reverse
vs. 5-4 Defense*

When to Use It:

● Use the *Slotback Reverse* only after the sweep play has been run successfully several times.

● It may be used against any style defense with slight blocking adjustments.

● Use this play when the defensive end to the reverse side becomes careless in his pursuit and is not watching for a possible reverse.

● Use this play when the offense has one or two guards who block well when pulling to lead a play.

● This play works well against teams who seem to be keying the halfbacks and ignoring the slotback as a ball carrier.

● This is a good play to use to the wide side of the field. The slotback will have a great deal of room to maneuver in open field against a limited number of defenders.

● Use the play often when the slotback is a better-than-average ball carrier.

● The quicker the defense pursues, the more chance the reverse has to be successful.

When Not to Use It:

● This play is probably not a good selection inside your own five-yard line. Because of the depth from which the slotback must run, there is a chance he could be tackled for a safety if the play is not executed properly.

● A slippery football, caused by rainy or snowy conditions, could hamper this play, as the football must be handled by three backs.

● Some coaches do not like to run reverse plays inside their opponent's five-yard line. If the play fails and several yards are lost, the chance of scoring is not as good.

● A slow slotback, noted more for blocking ability than running ability, could cause the play to fail.

Position Assignments:

Fake Sweep, Slotback Reverse
versus 5-4 Defense

LE—Block defensive tackle to the inside.

LT—Block linebacker your side.

LG—Pull as if to lead sweep; after two steps, turn and lead slotback on reverse.

C—Block middle guard.

RG—Pull as if to lead sweep; after two steps, turn and lead slotback reverse.

RT—Block defensive tackle.

Split End—Release downfield.

QB—Take snap; toss football to left halfback as he starts sweep; help lead reverse with guards.

RHB—Block defensive end to the sweep side.

LHB—Take pitch from quarterback; make handoff to slotback coming behind you; continue faking the sweep play.

SB—Open to the outside; come behind left halfback, taking football from him; follow blocks by guards and quarterback.

Coaching Points

Guards–The footwork of the guards is very important. If the reverse is going to the left as shown in Figure 6-1, the guards should open to the right with a lead step with the right foot. They should then step with the left foot and pivot away from the line of scrimmage, heading in the direction of the reverse.

If the left guard reaches the defensive end before the quarterback does, he must block him. If the quarterback has already blocked the end, the left guard must turn upfield and block the first defender to show. The right guard should block any defender who might happen to fire through the line and threaten the ball carrier. If no one comes, he should follow the left guard through the hole, looking for any defender in the area.

Quarterback—After taking the snap, the quarterback should open to his left by stepping at a 90-degree angle away from the line of scrimmage. He must take this step to avoid a collision with the left guard who is pulling. He then tosses the football to the left halfback and heads for the defensive end. If he reaches the defensive end first, the quarterback blocks him to the outside. If the left guard has already blocked the end, the quarterback leads through the hole looking for any defender in the area.

Left Halfback—Once he receives the toss from the quarterback, he places the football under his arm as if running the sweep. As he sees the slotback coming, the left halfback takes the football with both hands and hands it to him as the slotback comes behind him. Remember, it is the left halfback's responsibiliity to get the football to the slotback! After handing the football off, he should continue faking the sweep play. A good fake by the left halfback can make this play successful.

Right Halfback—The right halfback drives straight towards the defensive end on the right side. His block will keep the end from trailing the play and possibly making the tackle on the slot-back after he has received the handoff.

Slotback—The slotback opens the outside and begins his reverse pattern. Looking for the left halfback with the football, he adjusts his depth to meet the left halfback. He should receive the football no deeper than five yards from the line of scrimmage. Once the slotback has the ball, he looks for the blocks of the guards and the quarterback. If they block the defensive end to the inside, he must be ready to cut outside and run wide. If they block the end to the outside, he must be ready to cut up through the hole.

Left End, Center, and Both Tackles—These men need to be conscious of holding their blocks longer than usual. On a quick-hitting play a "brush" block is often sufficient. But on a reverse much more time is needed for the play to develop and they must work on sustaining their blocks until the play is over.

Play 7

Screen Pass to the Halfback

Basic Strategy:

Plays 7, 8, 9, 10, and 11 illustrate several different ways to execute screen passes, each with a different backfield pattern. The *Screen Pass to the Halfback* is a dropback screen pass. It is designed to take advantage of a defensive line (the end in particular) that puts pressure on the passer as he drops back to pass. The end and several other defensive linemen are allowed to penetrate the line of scrimmage and rush the passer. As the defenders get near, the quarterback tosses a short screen pass to the halfback on the left side. Three offensive linemen will block their men for two counts, then release them to rush the passer while they sprint to the left side and position themselves to block for the pass-receiving halfback. This play will continue to be successful as long as the defensive end rushes the passer hard.

60

Play Diagram:

Figure 7-1 shows the *Screen Pass to the Halfback* versus a 6-2 defense.

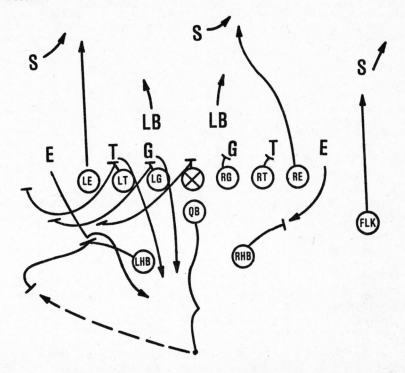

Figure 7-1   *Screen to the Halfback vs. 6-2 Defense*

When to Use It:

• Use this play when the defensive linemen, especially the end, put a hard rush on the quarterback as he drops back to pass.

• It is a good play to use if your team is noted for having a strong passing game and the defense knows it must get to the quarterback if it is to stop the long passes.

• Use this play if the left halfback is a good pass receiver.

• If the guards, tackles and center are mobile, quick and good downfield blockers, this play can turn into a long-gainer.

• Because the pass is short, weather conditions will have little effect on the play.

• Use this play if the defensive secondary is very strong and long passes have seldom been successful.

• This play can be adapted to take advantage of almost any type of defense.

• This play can be effective near an opponent's goal line, as the defensive line will be sure to rush the quarterback hard in this area.

• Use this play when running plays off-tackle and plays wide to the end's side have not been successful because of the aggressive nature of the defensive end.

When Not to Use It:

• If the defensive end plays "soft" and does not rush the quarterback on passing downs, the play will be difficult to execute.

• When backed up inside your own five-yard line, the play could be dangerous if not executed perfectly.

• If the offensive tackles, guards and center are big and slow, instead of quick and mobile, they may not be effective downfield blockers as needed for this play.

Position Assignments:

Screen to the Halfback versus 6-2 Defense

LE—Run deep pass pattern, taking safety on your side deep with you. After screen pass is completed, become downfield blocker.

LT—Block tackle for two counts; release to the left side and prepare to block downfield for the ball carrier.

LG—Block guard for two counts; release to the left side and prepare to block downfield for the ball carrier.

C—Check to see if a linebacker fires over you. If so, block him for two counts before releasing to the left side to block downfield for the ball carrier. If no linebacker fires, go ahead and release to the left side.

RG—Block guard over you. Work him to the right side as you block him.

RT—Block tackle over you. Work him to the right side, away from the area of the play.

RE—Run deep pass pattern, taking middle safety deep. After screen pass has been completed, become downfield blocker.

Flanker—Run deep pass pattern, taking safety on your side deep with you. After screen pass has been thrown, become a downfield blocker.

RHB—Block defensive end on your right side.

LHB—Block defensive end for one count. Make him release inside of you; sprint to your left 7-10 yards and turn facing the quarterback. Catch the screen pass and follow blocks of the center, left guard, and left tackle as they lead downfield.

QB—Set up in dropback passing position. As the defensive end approaches, toss a short pass to left halfback.

Coaching Points:

Quarterback—After taking the snap, the quarterback should drop back to his normal passing depth of 7-8 yards. Then, as the defenders on the left side get nearer, he must drop back several additional steps, drawing the defenders deeper into the backfield away from the area where the pass will be caught. As he drops back, the quarterback should be looking deep to the right side as if preparing to throw long to the flanker or right end. This will help draw attention away from the screen area. He must make sure the screen pass is thrown in a forward motion. If the left halfback should somehow make the mistake of setting up deeper in the backfield than the quarterback, the pass might be thrown at a backward angle and if dropped would be considered a fumble.

There is one situation which could develop as the play is executed that the quarterback must be trained to handle. If the defensive end *reads* the screen and goes with the left halfback the quarterback will not be able to throw the pass. In this case the left
halfback must forget the screen pass and head downfield as a pass
receiver. When this happens, the quarterback has two options: (1)
He can throw the ball away, making sure it is thrown towards a
potential receiver so that intentional grounding cannot be called.
(2) If possible, the best solution is to run towards the left halfback.
If the defensive end continues to cover the left halfback as he heads
downfield, the quarterback should have room to run for good yardage. If the defensive end stops coverage of the left halfback and
comes up to meet the quarterback, the quarterback should find the
left halfback uncovered downfield. Figures 7-2a, b & c illustrate
this movement.

Left Halfback—The left halfback must not set up too quickly.
He should make a good one-count block on the defensive end
before setting up for the screen pass. Once he sets up he should
raise his hands high if he is uncovered so the quarterback can find
him and know it is all right to throw the pass. If the defensive end
reads the screen pass and goes with the left halfback, the halfback
should break downfield. If the end covers him, the quarterback

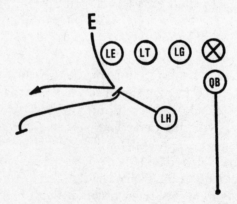

Figure 7-2a *Defensive end reads screen and goes with
left halfback.*

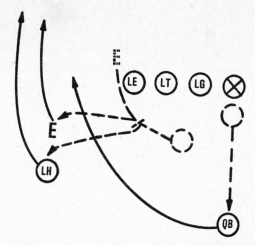

Figure 7-2b *Left halfback should release downfield. QB should run towards defensive end. If the end covers the left halfback, QB should run for good yardage.*

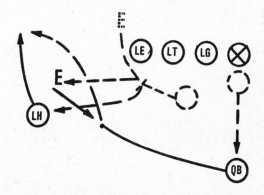

Figure 7-2c *Quarterback runs toward defensive end and end comes up to make tackle. QB now passes to left halfback.*

will have room to run for good yardage. If the end rushes toward the quarterback, the quarterback can then make a pass to the left halfback who should be left uncovered (see Figures 7-2a, b & c).

Left Tackle, Left Guard, Center—These men must make their two-count blocks on the line of scrimmage hard and tough. This will allow the quarterback plenty of time to set up and will add realism to the play. Once they set up the screen for the left halfback they must be sure they do not neglect to block any potential tackler. For them to allow a defender to run past and tackle the halfback as he catches the screen pass would be a cardinal sin!

Play 8

Screen to the Fullback

Basic Strategy:

The *Screen to the Fullback* is a play action pass that is quite different in its backfield execution from the dropback style of screen pass described in Play 7. This play has two strong points that make it successful: (1) The fake dive play will draw a number of defenders to the dive area. (2) The right tackle, right guard, and center will block for two counts, then allow the defenders on their side of the line to rush the quarterback, leaving the receiving area of the screen pass vacant. As with all screen passes, this play takes advantage of a hard rushing defensive line.

Play Diagram

The *Screen Pass to the Fullback* play is illustrated in Figure 8-1 and is diagrammed against a familiar 6-2 style defense.

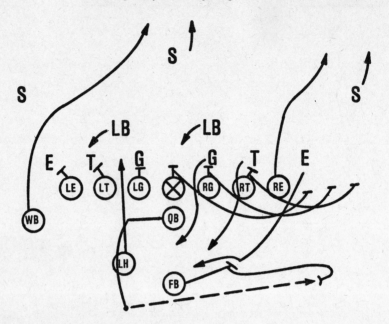

Figure 8-1   *Screen to the Fullback vs. 6-2 Defense*

When to Use It:

● Use this play after the halfback dive play has been run successfully several times.

● This play works well if the dive halfback is the team's best ball carrier and defensive men are keying his moves.

● There is no reason why this play cannot work well against any normal style defense with minor blocking adjustments.

● Utilize this play if the fullback has good hands for catching the football and is a good open-field runner.

● This play is a good choice if the long passing game has not been successful.

● Run this play when the defensive team believes the fullback to be only a power runner who is limited to straight-ahead dives and off-tackle plays.

● This play is good to call in short yardage situations when the defense is looking for a quick-hitting dive play.

● If the quarterback is good at faking, this play will probably be successful.

● Bad weather will not affect the execution of this play.

● Call this play anytime the defensive line (especially the end) penetrates hard across the line of scrimmage.

● This play works well if the defensive team is quick and reacts suddenly to the first movement of the offensive team.

When Not to Use It:

● Do not use this play if the defensive line (especially the end) plays soft and does not penetrate the line of scrimmage.

● If the fullback is primarily a blocker with no talent at catching the football, the play may be wasted.

● If the offensive team is inside its own five-yard line, the reverse action by the quarterback may force him into his own end zone and, if tackled there, would result in a safety.

Position Assignments:

Screen to the Fullback versus 6-2 Defense

LE—Block defensive end to the outside.

LT—Block tackle to the outside.

LG—Block guard over you.

C—Check for firing linebacker. If linebacker fires, block him for two counts, then release to the right side to set up screen.

RG—Block guard two counts; release to set up screen on the right side.

RT—Block tackle two counts; release to set up screen on right side.

RE—Release taking safety on your side deep. After pass is thrown to fullback, become downfield blocker.

Wingback—Release deep taking middle safety with you. After screen pass has been thrown, become downfield blocker.

LHB—Dive straight ahead, faking as if the quarterback gave you the ball.

FB—Block defensive end on the right side for one good count; set up behind screen blockers ready to receive pass from the quarterback.

QB—Fake dive play to the left halfback. Sprint 7-9 yards deep in the backfield and throw screen pass to the fullback.

Coaching Points:

Wingback and Right End—The wingback and right end must make sure they take their safety men as deep as possible. This removes them from the area of the screen pass and gives the fullback more running room once he catches the pass.

Right Tackle and Right Guard—The right tackle and right guard must make good, tough, two-count blocks on the line of scrimmage before releasing to set up the screen. Once they have set up the screen, they should never let any defender penetrate the area. They should listen for the fullback to holler "Go," then lead him downfield.

Fullback—The fullback should be sure to make blocking contact with the defensive end for one count before setting up for the screen pass. If there is no defensive man in the screen area, he raises both hands high as a signal to the quarterback to throw the pass. Once he has caught the football, he hollers "Go" so the screen blockers will know to start downfield. If the defensive end reads the screen and goes with the fullback, he should release downfield as explained in Figures 7-2a, b & c of the previous play.

Left Halfback—The left halfback must carry out his fake until the play is over or until he is sure the pass has been thrown. A good fake will draw several defensive men to his area and give the screen pass a better chance to be successful. Once he is sure the screen pass has been thrown, he becomes a downfield blocker.

Left End, Left Tackle, Left Guard—These men must hold their blocks on the line of scrimmage. They cannot let their defensive men penetrate and put pressure on the passer.

Quarterback—After making the fake to the left halfback, the quarterback sets up as quickly as possible. If the defensive end reads the screen and goes with the fullback, he runs towards the defensive end. If the end goes downfield with the fullback, the quarterback tucks the football under his arm and runs. If the defensive end rushes the quarterback, he tosses a pass to the fullback releasing downfield.

Play 9

Screen to the Tight End

Basic Strategy:

The *Screen to the Tight End* differs from the dropback-style screen pass in Play 7 and the play-action style screen pass in Play 8 in that it utilizes sprint-out action by the quarterback along with motion by the halfback. This creates a flood or overload pattern to the side away from where the screen will be set up. Most defensive teams are not coached to look for a screen to the tight end, and even if they are, it is difficult to read. Like all screens, this play takes advantage of overanxious defensive linemen. The halfback's motion and the quarterback's sprint action will cause reaction by the linebackers and rotation by the defensive secondary away from the screen area.

Play Diagram:

Figure 9-1 shows the *Screen to the Tight End* as executed against a 5-4 defense.

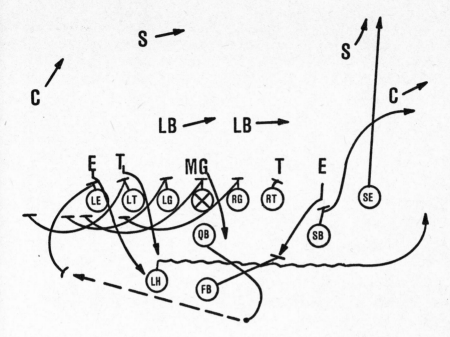

Figure 9-1 *Screen to the Tight End vs. 5-4 Defense*

When to Use It

- This play can take advantage of almost any normal defense.
- Use this play if the tight end is a good runner once he catches a pass.
- If motion by a halfback causes the defensive secondary to rotate towards the motion, this play will be successful.
- Look for the defensive end who comes hard across the line of scrimmage, then run this screen to his side.
- If the tight end has been used primarily as a blocker or as a deep receiver, this play could be quite successful.
- If the offense is built around the sprint-out run or pass play and the quarterback is a dangerous threat when running or passing, this play is a good call.
- Use this play to cut down backside pursuit of the quarterback by the defensive end when the quarterback runs the sprint-out play.

● If the quarterback generally likes to throw toward the side to which he sprints, this play could be a good change of pace.

● Since the pass is thrown only a short distance, weather will seldom be a factor in the play's success.

When Not to Use It:

● Do not use this play unless the defensive linemen are crossing the line of scrimmage hard and putting pressure on the quarterback.

● Select another play if the tight end is mainly a blocker with little or no pass-catching or running ability.

● As with most screen passes, think twice before calling this play inside the offensive team's five-yard line.

● Make sure several sprint-out run or pass plays have been called before using this play.

Position Assignments:

Screen to the Tight End versus 5-4 Defense

LE—Block end two counts; release him and set up to receive screen pass.

LT—Block tackle two counts; release him and set up screen to the left side.

LG—Check for linebacker firing. If he does, block him for two counts then set up screen on left side. If he doesn't, wait two counts and set up screen.

C—Block middle guard two counts; release him and set up screen on left side.

RG—Check for linebacker firing. If he does, block him for two counts and set up screen on left side. If he doesn't, wait two counts and set up screen.

RT—Block tackle to outside.

Slotback—Release towards defensive end. Block him one count and slide in flats as decoy pass receiver.

FB—Drive towards defensive end. After slotback blocks him one count, pick him up and continue blocking him until the play is over.

LHB—Go in motion as decoy pass receiver.

QB—Step with right foot at 45-degree angle and begin sprint-out pattern. On fourth or sixth step (depending on play timing), turn on left foot with back to line of scrimmage, get depth, and look to the screen side for the tight end. (See Figure 9-1 for the quarterback's correct path.)

Split End—Release downfield; take safety deep.

Coaching Points:

Quarterback—The quarterback should look at the receivers (slotback and split end) as he sprints out. He must make the defensive players think he has every intention of passing to one of the receivers or running to the sprint-out side. Once he makes his turn back towards the tight end, he should look for hands held high. This indicates the tight end is not covered and he should throw the pass. (See Figures 7-2a, b & c to review how the quarterback should react if the screen receiver is covered by the defensive end.)

Fullback—A good block on the defensive end on the sprint-out side is very necessary for the success of this play. The fullback should stay with him and, by all means, keep him away from the quarterback.

Left End—The left end must block aggressively against the defensive end for two counts. The more realistic he makes his block, the harder the defensive end will work to get past him and get at the quarterback. If the defensive end reads the screen and goes with the left end to the screen area the left end should react as described in Figures 7-2a, b & c. If he is alone as he sets up the screen, he raises both hands as an "all clear" signal to the quarterback. Once the pass has been caught, he hollers "Go" to the offensive linemen who have set up the screen.

Play 10

Screen to the
Slotback or Wingback

Basic Strategy:

Like most reverse plays, the *Screen to the Slotback or Wingback* is based on misdirection. Since the player who is to receive the screen pass comes from the opposite side of the offensive alignment it will be extremely difficult for the defensive players on the screen side to "read" the screen and cover the receiver. The defensive concentration will be directed at the quarterback-fullback-tailback fake of the off-tackle play.

Play Diagram:

This play is equally effective from a *slot* or *wing* formation. For illustration, we have diagrammed the play from the wingback formation as shown in Figure 10-1. The defense is a 6-2 alignment.

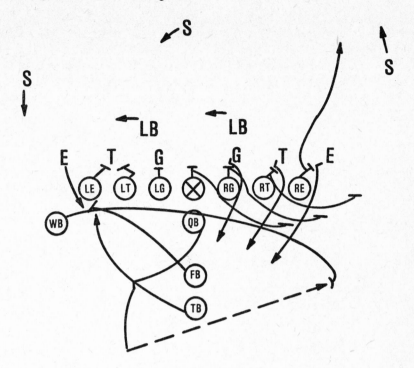

Figure 10-1 *Screen to the Wingback vs. 6-2 Defense*

When to Use It:

● Use this play when the defensive end on the side away from the off-tackle play crashes hard across the line of scrimmage.

● Use this play after the tailback off-tackle play has been successfully used.

● Weather conditions will seldom affect this play because of the nature of the short pass from quarterback to slotback or wingback.

● This play can be effective on short yardage situations such as second down and two yards to go for a first down. The defense will probably be expecting a power play into the line rather than a screen pass.

● This is a good pass to call if the defensive secondary has been effective in knocking down previous pass attempts.

● Use this play if the linebackers and safety men react quickly to the off-tackle power play.

● This play can be called often if the wingback or slotback is a good pass receiver and a good open field runner.

When Not to Use It:

● Inside the offensive team's five yard line, this play could be dangerous. Since the quarterback and the receiver would both have to operate in the end zone, this play could result in a safety or touchdown for the defense if not executed correctly.

● Do not call this play if the defensive end on the screen pass side plays soft and does not penetrate.

● Do not call this play until the tailback off-tackle play has been run successfully several times. The defense must be set up for the screen by showing the off-tackle play.

Position Assignments:

Screen Pass to the Wingback
versus a 6-2 Defense

LE—Block defensive tackle to inside.

LT—Check linebacker firing your gap. If linebacker doesn't fire, help end with defensive tackle.

LG—Block guard over you.

C—Check for linebacker firing. If none, move to screen area.

RG—Block guard two counts; move to screen area.

RT—Block tackle two counts; move to screen area.

RE—Block end one count to slow his charge; take safety on your side deep. After screen pass has been completed, become a downfield blocker.

FB—Block defensive end as if running off-tackle play.

TB—Lead-step with left foot parallel to line of scrimmage and turn into off-tackle hole. Make good fake as if the quarterback handed you the football.

WB—Sprint to opposite side of the field and set up for the screen pass.

QB—Make fake handoff to the tailback about four yards deep. Continue straight back and throw screen pass to wingback on the right side.

Coaching Points:

Wingback—At the snap of the ball the wingback starts immediately toward the screen area. He may have to pick his way through one or several defenders who have crossed the line of scrimmage and so must be careful that they don't knock him down and keep him from the screen area. If no one is covering him when he reaches the screen area, the wingback raises his hands as a signal to the quarterback that the area is clear. If a defensive player covers him, he reacts as described in Figure 7-2.

Fullback—A good aggressive block on the defensive end on the off-tackle play side is necessary to keep the end from pressuring the quarterback as he sets up to throw the screen pass. The tailback's fake into the off-tackle hole should make the fullback's block easier.

Tailback—The tailback takes one step parallel to the line of scrimmage with the left foot, then blasts into the off-tackle hole at full speed, faking as though he had the football. The tailback should continue to fake until he is tackled, until the whistle blows, or until he is sure the screen pass has been thrown. Remember, a good fake which distracts one defender is as good as making a block on that defender.

Quarterback—The quarterback reverses out, pivots around and makes a fake to the tailback at a depth of about four yards from the line of scrimmage. The quarterback should follow the tailback with his eyes, as if watching him run, while at the same time dropping back to a depth of eight to ten yards. He should look for the raised hands of the wingback, indicating he is open. If the wingback is covered, he should react as shown in Figure 7-2.

Left End, Left Tackle, Left Guard—These men must be sure to make their blocks as realistic as possible. The defense must believe the off-tackle play has been called. They should remember to hold their blocks as long as possible, giving the quarterback plenty of time to execute the screen pass.

Play 11

Screen to the Quarterback

Basic Strategy:

The *Screen to the Quarterback* is built on the belief that very few defensive teams are coached to look for a pass to the quarterback. Once the quarterback has taken the snap and has handed the football to another back, he is usually ignored. When executing this play, the quarterback must drift to the screen area as inconspicuously as possible while at the same time making sure he is ready to receive the pass by the time the left halfback is ready to throw it. Since every offensive team has some type of sweep play, this pass will be easy to incorporate into the playbook. Good defensive teams react quickly to stop a sweep play, and this can be a factor in the success of the screen pass.

Play Diagram:

The *Screen to the Quarterback* is shown in Figure 11-1 and is diagrammed against a 5-4 defense.

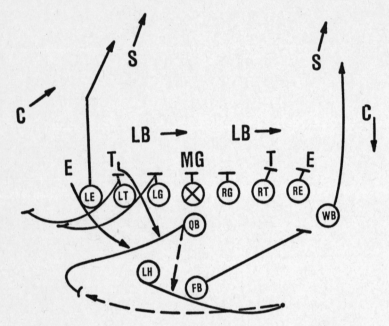

Figure 11-1   *Screen to the Quarterback vs. 5-4 Defense*

When to Use It:

• Select this play if the quarterback is a good runner, especially in the open field.

• This play works equally well against almost any defense.

• Call the play when the defensive linemen, especially the defensive end, crash hard across the line of scrimmage.

• Use this play if the defensive team reacts quickly to the sweep play around the end.

• Inclement weather will seldom harm this play since the pass is a rather short one.

● Use this play if the left halfback is an excellent ball carrier and the defensive people are "keying" heavily on him.

● Call this play after the sweep play has been run successfully several times.

● Use this play when it is noticed that the defensive players are ignoring the quarterback after he tosses the football to the left halfback on the sweep play.

● If the offensive team is noted for its powerful sweep play, the defensive team will probably be looking for it on the opening play of the game. In this case, the *Screen to the Quarterback* would be a perfect opening play call.

When Not to Use It:

● Do not use this play against a defense that has ends who play soft rather than rush hard across the line of scrimmage.

● This play could be dangerous to try if the offensive team is inside its own five-yard line. A safety could result if the play is not properly executed.

● Do not call this play until the threat of the sweep play has been established in the minds of the defensive players.

Position Assignments:

Screen to the Quarterback
versus the 5-4 Defense

LE—Release downfield, taking safety man deep.

LT—Block defensive tackle two counts; set up screen block to the left side.

LG—Check for firing linebacker. If he fires, block him two counts and release to set up screen block. If he doesn't, wait two counts and move to screen area.

C—Block middle guard. Do not let him penetrate and put pressure on the left halfback as he sets to pass.

RG—Block linebacker if he fires. If he doesn't fire, help the center or the right tackle with their blocks.

RT—Block defensive tackle.

RE—Block defensive end.

WB—Release, taking safety man deep.

FB—Block any defender outside the offensive right end who crosses the line of scrimmage.

LHB—Receive football from the quarterback. Start on normal sweep path but get slightly more depth. After several steps, stop and throw screen pass to the quarterback on the left side.

QB—Open to the left and toss football to left halfback. Move as quickly as possible to the screen area on the left side and wait for the pass from the halfback.

Coaching Points:

Fullback—The fullback must make sure he goes full speed towards the first defender outside the offensive end. He must not slow down after two or three steps as this will show that he is pass-blocking and will tend to give the play away.

Left Halfback—After taking the football from the quarterback, the left halfback places the football under the right arm just as he would when running the sweep. He should get slightly more depth than he normally would if he were actually running the sweep play (see Figure 11-2). After several steps, the left halfback should stop and look back towards the screen area for the quarterback to see if his hands are raised high indicating that he is open for the pass. If the quarterback is covered, it is probably best for the left halfback to look for daylight and try to run for as much yardage as possible by continuing the sweep play. It would be difficult to start back towards the screen area as is usually done with other screen passes.

Quarterback—After tossing the football to the left halfback, the quarterback should attempt to reach the screen area by drawing as little attention to himself as possible. He must not make a sudden, wild dash to the screen. Instead, he should move as though he is just getting out of the way of the play. After reaching the screen area he must check to be sure he is not covered. If the quarterback isn't covered, he raises both hands high as a signal to the halfback that the pass should be thrown. Once he has caught the football, the quarterback hollers "Go" to the screen blockers in front of him and follows their blocks downfield.

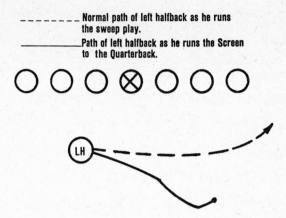

Figure 11-2

Play 12

Quick Pitch with Overshifted Backs

Basic Strategy:

The *Quick Pitch with Overshifted Backs* involves the sudden shift of three running backs which places them in good position to attack the defensive corner. Since the backs will leave the huddle and appear to be lining up in a normal backfield formation the defensive players will be forced to make quick defensive adjustments. If they don't do this properly, they will be outmanned at the point of attack. Because of the quick shift of the offensive backs the eleven defensive players will have to make their own adjustments with no time for help from their coaches. Most defensive players will not be able to do this correctly. The ball carrier will be running behind good blocking strength and should be able to turn the corner and start upfield quickly.

Play Diagram:

Figure 12-1 illustrates how the *Quick Pitch with Overshifted Backs* works.

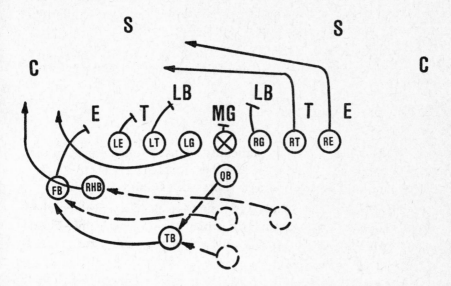

Figure 12-1 *Quick Pitch with Overshifted Backs vs. 5-4 Defense*

When to Use It:

● This play works well against any conventional defense

● This is an excellent play to use near the opponent's goal line (inside the 10-yard line), especially if the regular plays have failed.

● When a good drive stalls because of a penalty or some other technicality, this play can be the long-gainer needed to make the first down which keeps the drive going.

● Use this play if the defense is especially tough inside.

● Use this play if at least two good blocking backs are available.

● This is a good play to use if your scouting reports indicate that your opponent seems to have difficulty making adjustments to different offensive sets.

● Call this play often if you have a good, quick running back who can turn the corner well and is a good open field runner.

● Use this play if the defensive men on the outside (end and corner linebacker) have had success stopping the regular offensive plays that attack the outside.

● This is a good play to call if rain or other weather conditions have hampered the normal outside plays.

When Not to Use It:

● This play may have difficulty against a defensive team that intentionally sets its players wider than usual in an effort to stop the normal wide offensive plays or short passes into the flats area.

● This play may have little success against a well-coached defensive team that has scouted the play in a previous game. This is a good reason why the coach must select the right time to call a particular surprise play.

Position Assignments:

Quick Pitch with Overshifted Backs
versus 5-4 Defense

LE—Block defensive tackle.

LT—Block inside linebacker.

LG—Pull and lead the play around end.

C—Block middle guard.

RG—Block inside linebacker.

RT—Release downfield to block.

RE—Release downfield to block.

QB—Take snap and toss quick pitch to tailback.

FB—Break huddle and start towards fullback's normal position. Break left and line up three yards outside the left end. Block first defender inside.

RHB—Break huddle and start towards normal right halfback position. Break quickly to the left side and line up one yard outside the left end. Pull around fullback and lead play upfield.

TB—Start towards normal tailback position. Break and take new position slightly wider than normal left halfback position. Take toss from quarterback and follow blocks by left guard and right halfback.

Coaching Points:

Running Backs—You may start to show any backfield alignment (before shifting) such as the *Power "I,"Pro Set* and so on. Be sure to break the huddle and line up in the fake formation in plenty of time to move to the overshifted backs positions and still have ample time to be set for several seconds just before the ball is snapped. Failure to be set could cause an illegal procedure penalty. All backs should break for the new overshifted positions at a verbal command from the quarterback. Running backs, once they are in the overshifted positions, should be in a two-point stance with hands on the knees. (Some coaches may prefer their backs in three-point stances.)

The ball carrier should run to daylight and not be confined to one particular hole to hit. However, he should follow his blocking as long as possible, then break to the opposite side of the field and pick up his downfield blockers.

Quarterback—As the running backs approach their "fake" positions, call some type verbal command so that they will shift all at the same time. Be sure they are set in their new positions before calling for the snap so that no illegal procedure penalty will be called.

Right End and Right Tackle—Downfield blocking is an absolute necessity if a team is to be a consistent winner. These two players have no on-the-line blocking assignment. They must sprint downfield and block the safety men or any other defenders who threaten the ball carrier.

Play 13

The Shoestring Play

Basic Strategy:

The Shoestring Play is an excellent play that takes advantage of a team that lingers in the defensive huddle or is not alert as the offensive team breaks their huddle. There are two ways to run this play:

1. After completing the previous play, all offensive players pass within fifteen yards of the football that has been marked ready for play by the official (the rule book requires that players come within this distance of the ball). The players then suddenly take positions to the left (or right) of the football as shown in the following diagram. Since no huddle is used, this play must be called in advance in the previous huddle. When all players are set and still, the center picks up the football and tosses it to the halfback who is waiting behind a wall of blockers.

2. The offensive team huddles and *The Shoestring Play* is called. The players break the huddle and sprint to the line of

scrimmage lining up 10-15 yards to the left (or right) of the football. The center, who has left the huddle early and is waiting over the football, suddenly picks the ball up and tosses it to the waiting halfback.

This play forces 11 defensive players to have to make decisions concerning adjustment. Some defensive teams will be so surprised that they will ignore the strange formation completely. Other defensive teams will split up with several players going to the new formation and others remaining in their old defensive positions. Regardless of the defensive adjustments the players are sure to be somewhat confused and unsure of their defensive responsibliities.

Play Diagram:

Figure 13-1 shows *The Shoestring Play*. No defensive players have been placed in the diagram because there is no way to be sure how the defense will adjust.

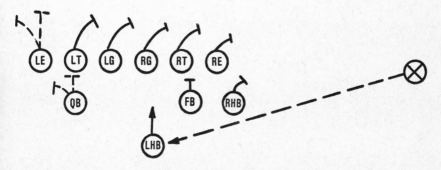

Figure 13-1 *The Shoestring Play*

When to Use It:

• This play can be called regardless of the style of defense being used.

• This play can be used in long or short yardage situations.

• Use this play against a defensive team that huddles after each play.

● Call this play against a defensive team that seems to be unable to make defensive adjustments on the field.

● Use this play when a good open field runner is available.

● This is a good play to use on the goal line if regular offensive plays are unsuccessful.

● This can be an especially effective play if the offensive players, linemen included, are quick.

● Call this play to the side of the weakest and least experienced defensive players.

● Use this play if the regular offensive plays have had little success.

● This play is a good call near the end of the first half. If successful, it could lead to a touchdown or field goal that could demoralize the defensive team just before the half.

When Not to Use It:

● This play could be risky inside the offensive team's five-yard line if the center's toss isn't accurate.

● This play may not be successful against an alert defensive team that is well coached in making adjustments.

Position Assignments:

Exact blocking assignments cannot be determined because there is no way to tell how the defensive players will react to *The Shoestring Play*. Therefore, players must be taught to block "an area" rather than a particular defensive player.

LE—Block first defender outside. If none, lead downfield.

LT—Block first defender inside.

LG—Block first defender inside.

C—Huddle over the football *before* the other offensive players take their positions. Once the other 10 players are set, pick up the football and toss it to the halfback.

RG—Block first defender inside.

RT—Block first defender inside.

RE—Block first defender inside.

QB—Line up behind the left tackle. Block first man to the outside. If none, lead downfield.

RHB—Line up just outside the right end. Block first defender inside.

FB—Line up behind right tackle. Lead straight downfield.

LHB—Line up behind right guard about seven yards deep. Take toss from the center and follow blockers.

Coaching Points:

All offensive players must be reminded that a key point in running *The Shoestring Play* successfully is that the play must be set up and executed quickly. Therefore, all players must reach their assigned positions at approximately the same time (except the center, who must set up first). If one player is a few seconds late in reaching his assigned position, the play will be delayed and the defense will have more time to consider proper coverage for the new formation.

Since the left halfback is the only offensive player in position to see the other 10 players, he should call for the center's toss as soon as he sees that all players are in position and have been still for the proper length of time.

All blockers must block the *nearest* defender rather than searching for a particular man to block. Never pass by any potential tackler!

Once the center has tossed the football to the halfback he must sprint downfield and block. He should also work daily on his toss to the halfback. Remind him that he must pick up the football and toss it all in one motion. Once he picks the ball up it is "live."

Play 14

Ten-Man Shift, Fullback Pass

Basic Strategy:

Unless the defensive team is exceptionally well coached the *Ten-Man Shift, Fullback Pass* can cause enough confusion among its players to allow a good gain by the offense. The nature of the play demands that the defenders react suddenly to the shifting of the 10 offensive players and that they make the proper adjustments.

In executing this play, the center must break the huddle first and take his position on the line of scrimmage. Then the other 10 players approach the line, but just before taking their stances, they shift to new positions 6-10 yards from the football. The ball is snapped to the fullback who tosses a short pass to the left halfback. The left halfback follows the blocking of his four teammates in front of him. Having several players shift to the right as well as to the left tends to divide the defensive team and gives the ball carrier fewer defenders to evade.

Play Diagram

Figure 14-1 illustrates the *Ten-Man Shift, Fullback Pass* play. No defense is shown as it is not possible to determine how the defensive players will align themselves.

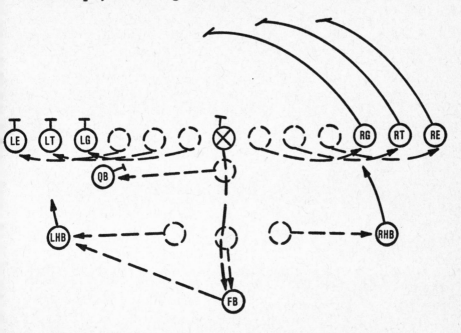

Figure 14-1 *Ten-Man Shift, Fullback Pass*

When to Use It:

● This is a good play selection for the opening play of the game.

● Call this play against any opponent regardless of their normal defensive alignment. The defense must adjust to a new alignment to try to stop this unusual offensive formation.

● Use this play against a weak defensive end, tackle, or corner linebacker.

● This is a good play if the left halfback is a good open field runner.

● This play works well against an inexperienced defensive team.

● This play can be called on any down. It can even be effective on fourth down, especially when your team is across the opponent's 50 yard line.

● Weather should not affect this play in any way.

● This play can be especially effective if the fullback has had passing experience.

● This is a good play to call near the opponent's goal line.

When Not to Use It:

● Do not use this play inside the offensive team's five-yard line until the risk of a possible safety is considered by the coaching staff.

● This play may fail to gain ground if used against an experienced defensive team that adjusts well to any new alignment.

Position Assignments:

LE—Approach line of scrimmage; shift to new position about 8-10 yards from the football. Block nearest defender in your area.

LT—Approach line of scrimmage; shift to new position about 7-9 yards from the football. Block nearest defender in your area.

LG—Approach line of scrimmage; shift to new position about 6-8 yards from the football. Block nearest defender in your area.

C—Break huddle early. After others have shifted, snap football to fullback. Block nearest defender in your area.

RG—Approach line of scrimmage; shift to new position 6-8 yards from the football. Block downfield.

RT—Approach line of scrimmage; shift to new position 7-9 yards from the football. Block downfield.

RE—Approach line of scrimmage; shift to new position 8-10 yards from the football. Block downfield.

QB—Approach line of scrimmage. All players except center will shift on your command. Take new position one yard back and one yard to the inside of the left guard. Block inside.

LHB—Approach normal halfback position; shift to new position behind left tackle and about 6 yards deep. Take pass from fullback and follow blockers.

FB—Approach normal fullback position; shift back 3-4 yards. Take snap and toss pass to left halfback.

RHB—Approach normal halfback position; shift to new position behind right tackle. Block downfield.

Coaching Points:

Offensive Linemen—All offensive linemen, except the center, must approach the line of scrimmage in unison and shift to their new positions at the same time for the play to be effective. As the linemen reach the line of scrimmage (before shifting) they should be in a two-point stance. Once the tackles and guards take a three-point stance, they are not allowed to move. We also advise their taking a two-point stance *after* they have shifted. Since there is no way to predict the defensive adjustment to this surprise play, the left end, left tackle and left guard must block the first defender in their area who is a threat to make the tackle.

Right Halfback—Although this man could be placed on the left side and used as a blocker, we feel he is more important as a decoy on the right side. His presence will draw several defenders to the right side of the offensive line.

Fullback—Just before calling for the snap the fullback should observe the general defensive alignment. He must watch for these points:

1. Did the defense adjust at all or just sit in their normal defense?
2. Did all the defenders go to one side?
3. Was the middle area over the center left vacant?
4. Could the fullback have run the football for good yardage rather than pass to the left halfback?

If the fullback remembers the answers to these four questions, perhaps the play can be called later in the game using another option such as the fullback running up the middle.

Play 15

Double Screen Pass

Basic Strategy:

The *Double Screen Pass* is a good play to call after the *Screen Pass to the Halfback* (see Play 7) has been called. Most teams are coached to react to a screen pass to one side, and many teams defend the screen quite well. The *Double Screen Pass* is designed to take advantage of these defensive teams by giving them the screen look to the defensive right side but throwing a delay screen to the defensive left side. In executing this play, the right side of the offensive team must hold their blocks slightly longer than the left side before setting up their screen. A good acting job is necessary by the quarterback and left halfback for the play to run smoothly.

Play Diagram:

This play, like all others in this book, can be run from many different formations. In Figure 15-1 the *Double Screen Pass* is

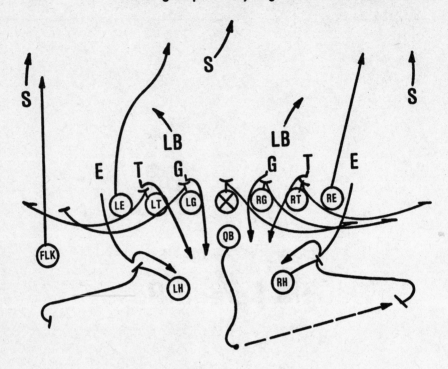

Figure 15-1 *Double Screen Pass vs. 6-2 Defense*

shown from a split backfield formation with a flanker to the left side. The play is drawn against a 6-2 defense.

When to Use It:

● As with all screen passes, this play works well against a weak defensive end.

● The play can be effective against almost any style defense.

● Use the play if *two* good open-field running halfbacks are available so that the defense cannot key on one halfback's side.

● Because the pass is a short one, this play can be used in any type weather.

● Use this play against a hard-charging defensive line.

● Use the play if good mobile guards and tackles are available on offense as the play demands movement by the offensive linemen.

● Call this play if the defensive secondary is strong and the long passing game has been having difficulty.

● Call the play if the screen pass to the left halfback has been used successfully. The defense will probably be looking for it again, making the *Double Screen Pass* more likely to be successful.

● If the screen pass to the left halfback has *not* been successful, it could be because the defense has been coached to defend it. Therefore, the *Double Screen Pass* could come as a surprise to the defense and become a long gainer.

When Not to Use It:

● Do not use the play if the defensive line plays soft and does not charge hard across the line of scrimmage.

● The play can be risky inside the offensive team's five-yard line.

● A prevent type defense may be able to react quickly to the play.

Position Assignments:

LE—Release downfield taking middle safety man deep. Block downfield after the play has developed.

LT—Pass block for two counts; set up screen block to left side.

LG—Pass block for two counts; set up screen block to left side.

C—Check for firing linebacker. Pass-block (if linebacker fires) for three counts; set up screen block to the right side.

RG—Pass-block for three counts; set up screen block to the right side.

    RT—Pass-block for three counts; set up screen block to right side.

    RE—Release downfield, taking safety man on your side deep. Block downfield after play has developed.

    Flanker—Release downfield; taking safety man on your side deep. Block downfield after the play has developed.

    LHB—Block defensive end one count. Set up fake screen to the left side.

    RHB—Block defensive end for two counts. Set up in screen area to the right and receive screen pass from the quarterback.

    QB—Drop back as if to pass downfield. Look deep to the right side as you drop back. As screen to the *left* side begins to form, look in that direction as if to toss a screen pass to the left halfback. Then turn suddenly and toss a screen pass to right halfback on the right side.

Coaching Points:

    Timing is the key factor in the success of this play. The players must be drilled and drilled, until the screen on the left side forms slightly before the screen on the right side forms. In other words, the defense should be attracted to the left side of your offense first and the right side second. All players on the left side of the offense must carry out their screen assignments at full speed even though they know the pass will not come their way.

    The quarterback must be taught not to take a loss if the screen to the right halfback is not open. Since a number of defensive linemen are rushing him it is probably best to get rid of the football by throwing it towards an eligible receiver but not so near a defender that it might be intercepted.

Play 16

Fake Option, Wingback or Slotback Reverse

Basic Strategy:

The *Fake Option, Wingback or Slotback Reverse* is an excellent misdirection play which evolves from one of football's most popular plays—the option play. The defensive players first see the inside fake by the fullback and must react to him. Then the defenders see the quarterback coming down the line of scrimmage and expect him to keep the ball or make a pitch to the trailing halfback. But instead the pitch goes to the wingback (or slotback or tight end with slight changes in formation) who is moving in the opposite direction. This play is very effective because the defensive players actually see the football pitched in the direction of the trailing halfback as done in the normal option play. Few defensive players will expect the wingback to be the ball carrier once the play starts.

Play Diagram:

Figure 16-1 illustrates the *Fake Option, Wingback Reverse* against a 5-4 defense. With slight alterations in formation a slotback, tight end or even a split end can carry out the assignments of the wingback.

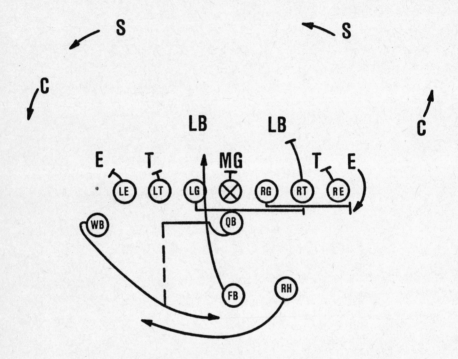

Figure 16-1   *Fake Option, Wingback or Slotback Reverse vs. 5-4 Defense*

When to Use It:

- Use this play if the offensive team is known to be a strong option team.
- Use the play against a weak defensive end.
- Use the play against a defensive team which reacts quickly to the first movement of the offense.

● Call the play if a fast wingback is available who is a good open field runner.

● Use this play if the defense has stopped the normal option play.

● Call this play towards the wide side of the field.

● This is a good long yardage play (such as third down and nine yards to go).

● Call this play near the opponent's goal line. Since the defense must react quickly to the fullback's fake and the quarterback's option move, the play can develop into an easy score.

● This play works well if the quarterback is a good ball handler and running threat.

When Not to Use It:

● The play may not be too effective if the option play is not among the normal plays used by the offensive team.

● If the weather is bad enough to threaten the regular option play pitch, it would also affect this play.

● Because of the possibility of a fumble during the pitch, some coaches may choose not to use this play near their own goal line.

Position Assignments:

Fake Option, Wingback Reverse
versus 5-4 Defense

LE—Block defensive end.

LT—Block defensive tackle.

LG—Pull; lead play.

C—Block middle guard toward pitch side (away from reverse side).

RG—Pull and lead the play. Watch for defensive end and block him to outside if possible. If end rushes tight to inside, block him inside and ball carrier will go outside.

RT—Block linebacker over you.

RE—Block tackle to your inside.

FB—Fake dive inside. Block linebacker if he does not tackle you.

RHB—Take pitch route.

QB—Reverse out; fake handoff to fullback; continue down line of scrimmage and pitch to wingback.

WB—Open to the outside and reverse direction. Run inside right halfback, taking pitch from quarterback.

Coaching Points:

Left Guard and Right Guard—As the left and right guards pull they should look for the first defender to cross the line of scrimmage and block him. If no one has crossed the line of scrimmage before they get to the defensive end they should let the lead guard block the end and the trailing guard turn upfield inside the block. The guards must not string the play out. Remember, the wingback is following their blocks and they must turn him upfield as soon as possible. The left guard, as he pulls, must be careful not to run into the quarterback, who will be going in the opposite direction.

Fullback—The fullback's fake is one of the most important parts of the play. He is the first man the defensive players will notice and he must draw several players to his area thinking he has the football. If he is not tackled (and he should be if he has made a good fake), he must block the inside linebacker or any other defender in the area.

Right Halfback—The right halfback sprints at full speed and must carry out the option fake. He should get a little more depth than usual because the wingback must run inside him to take the pitch. The right halfback should carry out his option route and continue to attract attention even after the pitch has been made to the wingback.

Quarterback—A good fake to the fullback is necessary. Then the quarterback must carry out the option play route even after he has made the pitch to the wingback. He must be careful, as he starts the play, not to run into the left guard as he pulls. This is one reason why we like a reverse pivot after the quarterback takes the snap and starts the fullback fake. Be sure the quarterback's pitch to the wingback is not too hard. This might result in the football hitting the shoulder pads and a fumble occurring. Make the pitch soft. The quarterback should allow the wingback to catch it in his hands rather than having to trap it against his body.

Wingback—As you start your reverse be sure to come inside the right halfback, not behind him. Stay a depth of about five yards from the quarterback. After taking the pitch, look for the two pulling guards and follow their blocks.

Part IV

Penetrating the Defensive Secondary with Surprise Passes

Play 17

Screen Pass, Double Pass

Basic Strategy:

The *Screen Pass, Double Pass* is designed to confuse defensive backs by forcing them to come forward as they see a short screen pass being thrown to the halfback. This leaves their deep pass defense areas uncovered enabling the split end to decoy his way into the vacated area and receive a pass from the halfback. This play should be set up in advance by throwing a screen pass to the halfback early in the game.

Play Diagram:

Figure 17-1 illustrates the *Screen Pass, Double Pass*.

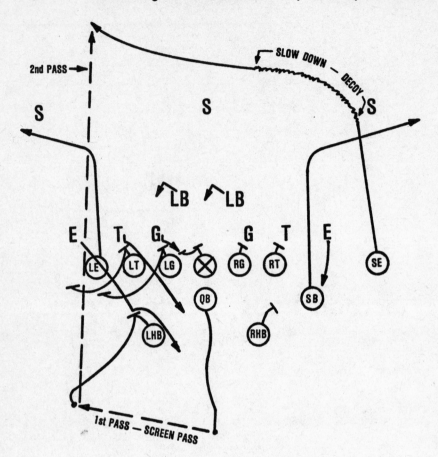

Figure 17-1 *Screen Pass, Double Pass*

When to Use It:

- Use this play against any conventional defense.
- Call this play when it is noticed that the defensive backs are reacting rapidly to the screen pass whenever it has been called.
- Use the play when a defensive back fails to watch for a pass receiver coming into his territory from across the field.
- If any, or all, of the defensive backs are playing near the line of scrimmage, the play has a great chance of being successful.

● Use the play against any defensive back who continually allows receivers to get behind him.

● This play can be called any time during the game but will have a better chance to fool the defense if the regular screen pass (with no double pass) has been thrown at some time during the game. (*Note*: If the offensive team is known to throw screen passes every game, the defense is certain to be on the lookout for the screen. Therefore, the *Screen Pass, Double Pass* would make a good opening game play.)

● Use this play during any down. A second down and one yard to go for a first down is a good situation in which to throw the pass, as the defensive backs will probably be near the line of scrimmage.

When Not to Use It:

● Do not attempt this play if the defense is consistently good at reading your screen. Once the halfback catches the football, he must have time to throw his pass to the split end.

● Some coaches will not wish to use this play when backed up inside their own five-yard line because the screen pass would have to be caught, and the second pass thrown, from inside the end zone. However, the play can work from here if the coach is willing to gamble on avoiding a possible safety or a touchdown by the defense on an interception.

Position Assignments:

Screen Pass, Double Pass versus 6-2 Defense

LE—Run short down and out pattern, making sure safety man on your side covers you.

LT—Bump defensive tackle; move into screen pass blocking position.

LG—Bump defensive guard; move into screen pass blocking position.

C—Check linebackers; if none fires, block left guard's man after left guard releases.

RG—Block defensive guard.

RT—Block defensive tackle.

Split End—Decoy to far side of the field to receive pass from the halfback.

QB—Drop back slightly deeper than usual; look as if to pass to the right side; turn and throw screen to left halfback.

Slotback—Run down and out pattern to right side.

RHB—Block defensive end.

LHB—Set up to pass block; bump defensive end one count; release quickly to the left 7-10 yards from the quarterback; catch screen pass 5-7 yards behind line of scrimmage; throw second pass to split end deep downfield.

Coaching Points:

Left End—It is important that the left end attracts the attention of the safety man on his side and makes the safety cover him until the screen pass is thrown. The safety must not be allowed time to see the split end decoying across field to a position behind him.

Left Tackle and Left Guard—Their screen blocks must be good enough to keep any defensive player from tackling the halfback before he throws his pass or from batting the pass down. As they set up their screen block they should be sure to block the first defender who threatens the halfback.

Split End—The split end must release downfield at full speed for seven to nine yards. As soon as the quarterback starts his screen pass toss to the halfback, the split end breaks his stride and slows down slightly. This gives the defensive backs the idea that he is no longer a vital part of the play. As the secondary defenders sprint towards the halfback, he cuts across the field and resumes running at full speed. He goes deep and begins looking for the pass from the halfback. If he has decoyed well, he should be all alone!

Left Halfback—Remember that the screen pass must be successful before the second pass can be thrown. The left halfback

should set up in his pass-blocking position and give the defensive
end a good one-count block. He then releases and sprints to his
left, being sure to set up well behind the line of scrimmage. Once
he catches the pass from the quarterback, he looks quickly
downfield for his split end. If the split end is wide open be sure that
the left halfback doesn't ruin the play by throwing the ball too hard
or making him have to run for it. He must throw him an easy-to-
catch pass, for there is little the defensive backs can do at this point
to destroy the play.

Play 18

Halfback Dropback Pass

Basic Strategy:

The *Halfback Dropback Pass* is one of the simplest of the surprise plays and one of the easiest to execute, but it can be one of the most effective. It is based on the idea that at the instant the quarterback has given the football to another back, the threat on a pass is eliminated. To fully utilize this play, it is necessary to have a running back who is a capable passer. Since most backs are usually good athletes, one with passing ability shouldn't be hard to find. The *Halfback Dropback Pass* will add another dimension to any team's passing game.

Play Diagram:

The *Halfback Dropback Pass* is shown in Figure 18-1 against a 5-4 defense. The pass routes shown in the diagram can, of course, be changed depending on the defense and the preference of the offensive team.

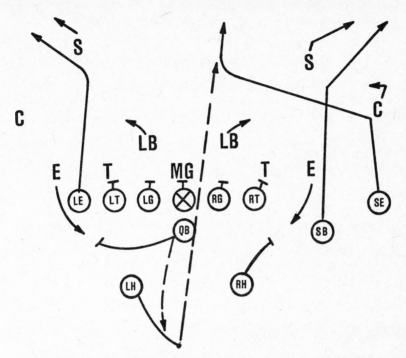

Figure 18-1 *Halfback Dropback Pass vs. 5-4 Defense*

When to Use It:

• Use this play if the defensive backs come up or stop coverage of receivers as soon as the quarterback gets rid of the football.

• Use the play if the quarterback is a good ball handler and runner but is no better at passing than one of the running backs.

• Call the play if a variation in the passing attack is needed.

• Use the play when a good passing halfback is available.

• Call the play if the defensive backs are inexperienced or are generally regarded as poor defenders.

● Use this play when good receivers with ability to get open are in the lineup.

● This play can be effective against most any defensive alignment.

● Try this play if the regular quarterback's passing game has not been successful.

● The play can be used on any down.

● It is a good goal line play.

● Use the play if the quarterback has an injury which limits his throwing ability.

● Call the play if a second or third string quarterback is in the game and he is not an experienced or accurate passer.

When Not to Use It:

● The play cannot be used unless a running back with some passing ability is on the team.

● There is no need to call this play and show it to future opponents if the regular quarterback is passing well.

● Never call a play like this if the offensive team has a big lead or is trailing by a large score. Save it for that close game when the play can mean the difference between winning and losing.

Position Assignments:

Halfback Dropback Pass versus 5-4 Defense

LE—Run pass route, taking safety man down and out.

LT—Block defensive tackle.

LG—Check for firing linebacker.

C—Block middle guard.

RG—Check for firing linebacker.

RT—Block defensive tackle.

RE—(Split end) Run deep pattern up the middle of the field.

SB—(Slot back) Run down and out pattern.

RHB—Block defensive end.

QB—Toss football to left halfback and block defensive end.

LHB—Take football and drop back to spot where quarterback normally throws from. Look for open receiver.

Coaching Points:

Quarterback—After taking the snap, the quarterback opens to the side of the back who is to throw the pass. He tosses him the football, keeping in mind that the back will be going in a "backward" direction (away from the quarterback). The quarterback blocks the defensive end with the usual backfield style pass block. He meets the defensive end as near the line of scrimmage as possible. The quarterback must never let the end force him deep in the backfield where he will get in the way of the halfback as the halfback attempts to find a receiver and complete the pass.

Left Halfback—The left halfback's first step should be at a 45-degree angle away from the line of scrimmage. He should receive the tossed football from the quarterback as he retreats to a passing depth of from seven to nine yards. Knowledge of the defensive secondary alignment will help him pick out his open receiver. If no receiver is open, he should run with the football or throw an "incomplete" pass. This is done by passing the football into an area near enough to an eligible receiver so that intentional grounding will not be called, yet far enough away so that no defender in the area can make an interception. Be sure to have the halfback practice passing every day to improve arm strength and passing accuracy.

Play 19

Halfback Sweep Pass

Basic Strategy:

The *Halfback Sweep Pass* differs from the *Halfback Dropback Pass* (Play 18) in that it is definitely intended to look like a running play. At the last second, the ball carrier passes to the split end or any other receiver who can be worked into the pattern. This play is easy to install because every offense has a sweep or end run play. The play can be used with any style offensive set. It is designed to take advantage of fast reacting safety men who come up quickly on wide running plays.

Play Diagram:

Figure 19-1 shows the *Halfback Sweep Pass* versus a 5-4 defense. The *Power "I"* offensive set offers good blocking protection for the ball carrier/passer. The split end is the primary receiver while the tight end offers an alternate choice if the split end is covered.

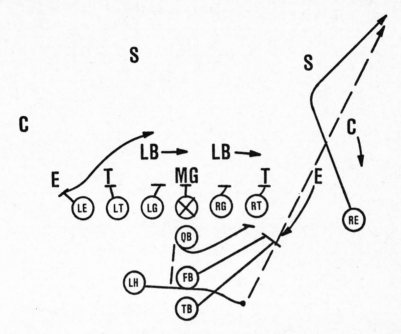

Figure 19-1 *Halfback Sweep Pass*

When to Use It:

- Use this play after the sweep play has been run successfully several times.
- Use it against a weak secondary defense.
- The play works well against defensive backs who come up quickly to stop the sweep play.
- Use the play if a good throwing halfback is available.
- The play is a good call on long *or* short yardage situations.
- The play can be called deep in the offensive team's territory provided the passer understands how to get rid of the football if the receivers are covered.

● Use the play if a receiver is available who can disguise his pass-receiving intentions and make it appear as if he is coming downfield to block.

● Use the play if the regular passing game hasn't been successful.

● Utilize the play if the regular quarterback is injured or otherwise out of the game and the substitute quarterback isn't a good passer.

When Not to Use It:

● Do not use this play in a game until the passing halfback has had sufficient practice time passing to his receiver under game-type conditions.

● It is best to save the *Halfback Sweep Pass* until the sweep play itself has been run several times. However, if a team is noted for running a successful sweep, the play could be used very early in the game.

● Do not try to use the play unless a halfback with some passing ability is available on the team.

● The play may not be successful against a pass-conscious secondary defense whose players do not come up quickly.

Position Assignments:

Halfback Sweep Pass versus a 5-4 Defense

LE—Bump the defensive end. Drag shallow across the middle behind the inside linebackers.

LT—Block the defensive tackle.

LG—Check for firing linebacker. Can pull if you (the coach) prefer.

C—Block middle guard.

RG—Check for firing linebacker. Can pull if you (the coach) prefer.

RT—Block defensive tackle.

RE—(Split end) Run deep in-and-out route.

FB and TB—Block defensive end and any other defenders rushing from the outside.

QB—Toss football to left halfback. Help the fullback and tailback block any defenders outside the defensive tackle.

LHB—Take football and start normal sweep route. Toss pass to the split end (or the left end dragging across the middle).

Coaching Points:

Split End—The split end starts towards the deep safety on his side. He runs at him as if to block him, then turns sharply to the outside looking back for the pass from the halfback.

Left Halfback—The left halfback must be drilled to make the sweep play look as normal as possible before turning it into a pass play. He should take the football and tuck it under his arm just like he does on the sweep play. As he gets near the point of his sweep where he is behind the right tackle area he should dip slightly away from the line of scrimmage. This will give him a little more room in which to slow down and find his receiver. Work with this player to help him find his secondary receiver (left end) in case the split end isn't open.

Play 20

Throwback to Quarterback Pass

Basic Strategy:

It is very natural for the defensive players to have their eyes on the quarterback when the ball is snapped and to continue to watch him until he hands the football to another back. But at that point the pattern changes. The quarterback is usually the forgotten man. The *Throwback to Quarterback Pass* takes advantage of this fact.

After making the handoff to the left halfback on an apparent halfback end sweep play, the quarterback swings to the outside, away from the widest defender. The halfback fakes an end sweep, stops, and throws back to the quarterback.

Play Diagram:

Figure 20-1 shows the *Throwback to Quarterback Pass* play against a 5-4 defense. As shown in the diagram the guards can either pull (as they probably do for the regular sweep play) or check for firing linebackers.

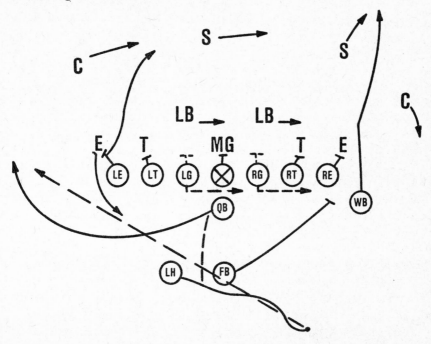

Figure 20-1 *Throwback to Quarterback Pass vs. 5-4 Defense*

When to Use It:

● This is an excellent play against a man-to-man defense where no defensive player is assigned to cover the quarterback.

● Use the play after the sweep has been run successfully several times.

- It is a good call against a weak defensive secondary.
- It is a good call against an inexperienced team.
- Use the play if a halfback with passing ability is available.
- This play is a good call if the quarterback is a good athlete (most quarterbacks are) who can catch the football.
- Call this pass when the defensive players react quickly to the flow of the sweep play.
- The play can be used on any down.
- Use the play when the football is located at any position on the field if the passing halfback is aware of what to do with the football in case the quarterback is covered by a defender.
- This play can be used on the opening play of the game provided the offensive team is noted for running a sweep play often.

When Not to Use It:

- Do not use it against a slow-reacting defensive secondary.
- Do not use it if the defensive team is exceptionally well coached and keeps an eye on the quarterback after he makes his handoff.
- The play will not be successful if a halfback with some passing ability isn't available.
- The play will probably not work well against a prevent-type defense.

Position Assignments:

Throwback to Quarterback Pass
versus 5-4 Defense

LE—Bump defensive end enough to keep him from rushing hard across the line of scrimmage and putting pressure on the passing halfback. Run pass route through the deep middle area, hopefully taking the cornerback or a safety man with you.

LT—Block defensive tackle.

LG—Can pull as he would probably do on a normal sweep play, or can check for firing linebacker.

C—Block middle guard.

RG—Can pull as he would probably do on a normal sweep play, or can check for firing linebacker.

RT—Block defensive tackle.

RE—Block defensive end.

WB—Release; take safety man deep.

FB—Sprint to the right end/wingback area. Block any defender to show.

LHB—Take pitched football from quarterback. Start sweep route. Pull up behind the right tackle area and throw pass to the quarterback sprinting down the left sidelines.

QB—Take snap and toss football to the left halfback. While attracting as little attention as possible, work to the outside of the defense and sprint downfield looking for a pass from the left halfback.

Coaching Points:

Left Halfback—The left halfback must make sure the play looks like the start of the regular sweep play by tucking the football under the right arm for several steps. As he nears the area behind the right tackle, he should get a little depth. This is necessary to give him time to stop, find the quarterback, and get the pass off to him. He should not throw to the quarterback if any defender is in the area. After making the pass, he should sprint to the left (in the direction of the pass) as a precaution against an interception.

Quarterback—When running the normal sweep play, the quarterback must observe the area where he will be running his pass route. He should find the best area to receive the pass (see Figures 20-2a, b & c). If there is no defender in the area, the quarterback must get as much depth as possible downfield. If a deep safety man is in the area he should cut his route short. If a

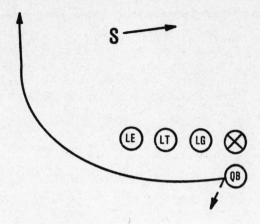

No defender in the area. Get as much depth as possible.

Figure 20-2a

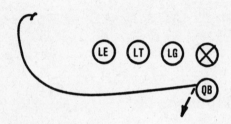

Deep defender in the area. Cut route short.

Figure 20-2b

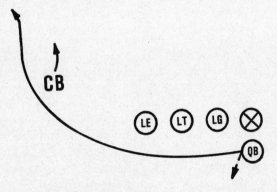

Cornerback in the short area. Run deep route behind the cornerback.

Figure 20-2c

cornerback is in the short area he should run a deep route, getting behind the cornerback.

Offensive Lineman—The offensive linemen use their aggressive pass-blocking techniques for this play rather than their dropback pass-blocking techniques. Remember, the play is supposed to look like a running play.

Play 21

Flea Flicker Pass

Basic Strategy:

The deceptive *Flea Flicker Pass* is based on the same principle as Play 20 (*Throwback to Quarterback Pass*) in that once the defensive players see a normal play (hook pass to the slotback) developing, they tend to forget all other potential ball carriers. This play will require as much timing as any surprise play described in this book, maybe more. The slotback must be a good athlete, for he will be called on to release from the line of scrimmage, run a pass route, catch the football, and lateral it to a teammate. If the normal slotback cannot meet these qualifications perhaps another player can be inserted for this particular play.

Play Diagram:

Figure 21-1 shows the *Flea Flicker Pass* against a 5-4 defense, but it can be equally effective against almost any defense.

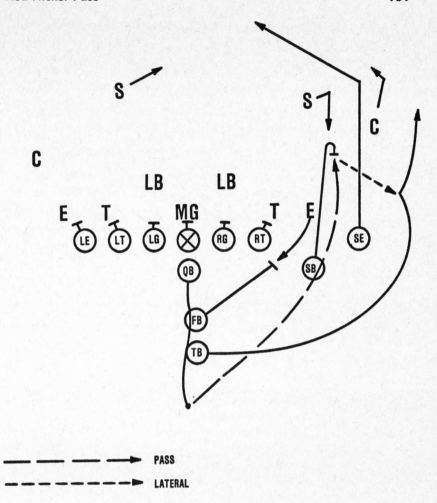

Figure 21-1 *Flea Flicker Pass*

When to Use It:

• This play can be very effective if the offensive team has good athletes at quarterback, slotback, and tailback.

• Use the play if the hook pass to the slotback is among the regular offensive plays that can be run successfully.

• Call the play to the side of the defense where the safety man and/or the cornerback seem to be the weakest.

• Use the play anywhere on the field, although it is not likely to be used near the opponent's goal line (the hook pass without the lateral may be enough to score).

• Use the play against defensive teams that react well to the path of the football. The pass to the slotback will draw attention to that area and away from the trailing tailback, who will eventually be the ball carrier.

• Use the play against the defensive back who likes to play several yards deeper than the receiver. This gives time for the slotback to catch the football and complete the lateral.

When Not to Use It:

• Do not use the play if the slotback isn't a good athlete (he must be able to catch a pass, then lateral successfully).

• Do not call the play inside the defensive team's eight-yard line. The hook pass itself, if completed, should be enough for a touchdown without risking a fumble.

• The play may have trouble being successful if the defensive back covering the slotback plays very tight man-to-man defense, which would not allow the slotback to complete the lateral after catching the pass.

• Because of the ball handling and timing needed for this play the coach should consider the weather (rain, snow) before choosing to call it.

• The play may not work against a spread-out, prevent-type defense.

Position Assignments:

Flea Flicker Pass versus 5-4 Defense

LE—Block defensive end.

LT—Block defensive tackle.

LG—Check for firing linebacker. If none, help another offensive lineman who needs blocking help.

C—Block middle guard.

RG—Check for firing linebacker. If none, help another offensive lineman who needs blocking help.

RT—Block defensive tackle.

Split End—Run route down and through the middle.

Slotback—Run hook route to depth of 8-10 yards. Catch pass, then lateral football to tailback coming to the outside.

QB—Drop back, throw hook pass to slotback.

FB—Make block on defensive end (this is a key block).

TB—Swing to the outside, taking a path that will bring you within 6-10 yards of the slotback as he catches the pass. Take lateral from slotback.

Coaching Points:

Split End—The split end runs his route so as to draw the deep safety man on his side away from the area of the lateral. This is best done by having the split end run towards him, making sure the safety covers him, then cutting towards the middle of the field.

Slotback—Since timing is very important, the slotback must position himself so that he can release off the line of scrimmage with a minimum of resistance. He should sprint to his hook area, 8-10 yards downfield. Once he stops his forward progress, he must come back towards the quarterback a step or two. This will help him get greater distance between himself and the defensive back covering him. The slotback must make sure he is not in too big a hurry to make the lateral as he must catch the pass first. The slotback should never take his eyes off the football as it is being passed to him. He must make the catch, *then* execute the lateral. The slotback must make the lateral to the tailback easy to catch. He should toss the football with a firm motion, yet not so hard that it will be difficult to catch or will bounce off the hard surface of the shoulder pads.

Fullback—The fullback must block aggressively on the defensive end. He should strike him low (between the knee and the belt area) so that he will keep his hands down and not be able to block the pass from the quarterback to the slotback.

Tailback—The tailback should release parallel to the line of scrimmage and turn upfield, attracting as little attention as possible. He must run his route so that he will come within 6-10 yards of the slotback after he makes his catch. He may need to adjust his running speed as the play develops so that he will be in the correct position to receive the lateral. Remember, he *must* be behind the slotback rather than in front of him for the lateral to be legal.

Play 22

End Around Pass

Basic Strategy:

The *End Around Pass*, if run from the overshifted formation as shown in the diagram, has three deceptive features: (1) The overshifted backfield gives the appearance that the play is designed to hit hard in the area of the off-tackle hole on the left side of the offense. (2) The reverse by the left end gives a misdirection look to the play. (3) The forward pass, thrown by the end, takes advantage of an already confused defensive secondary.

Play Diagram:

Figure 22-1 illustrates the *End Around Pass* as executed against a 5-4 defense.

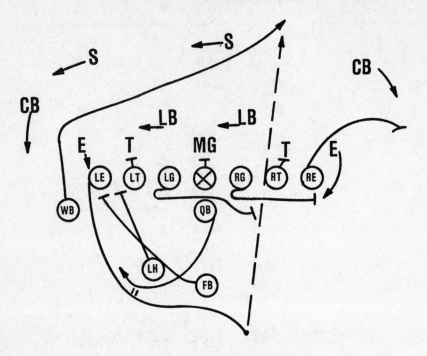

Figure 22-1 *End Around Pass*

When to Use It:

● Use the play after successfully running several plays toward the overshifted side of the offense.

● Use the play when the defense overshifts toward the strong side of the offense.

● It is a good play against a defensive team that reacts quickly to the first movement of the offensive team.

● This play should be used against a team with a weak pass defense.

● Call the *End Around Pass* if the reverse has already been run successfully.

● Use the play if the secondary defenders tend to overlook pass receivers once it appears that a running play is developing.

● Use this play if a tight end with passing ability is available.

● This is a good play against a defense which doesn't penetrate across the line of scrimmage quickly. (This will allow more time for the passer to locate his receiver.)

● The play can be used almost anywhere on the field.

● Use the play if the quarterback's passing plays haven't been successful.

● This play may have success against a short yardage defense where the defensive backs are closer to the line of scrimmage than usual.

When Not to Use It:

● Of course, the play cannot be used if no passing tight end is available.

● The play may not be successful against a defensive secondary that stays deep and rotates slowly.

● Because of the ball handling needed for the reverse and the long pass, you may not wish to call the play in adverse weather.

● It is seldom a good play selection against a prevent defense unless the secondary defenders in the prevent defense are quick to leave their assigned areas of coverage.

Position Assignments:

End Around Pass versus 5-4 Defense

LE—Open with the inside or outside foot, depending on the coach's preference. Sprint into the backfield, being sure to come *behind* the left halfback and the fullback. Take the handoff from the quarterback and take several steps as if running a reverse. Stop and throw to the wingback dragging deep across the field.

LT—Block defensive tackle.

LG—Open with left foot starting toward the left. Step with the right foot and reverse direction. Block first defender to threaten the passer.

C—Block middle guard.

RG—Open with the left foot starting toward the left. Step with the right foot and reverse direction. Block first defender to show (probably the defensive end).

RT—Block defensive tackle.

RE—Release on a short outside pattern, forcing the defensive back on that side to cover you.

LHB—Block defensive end.

FB—Help left halfback with defensive end or block any other defender to show.

QB—Open to the right. Sprint to the left as if on a quarterback roll-out play. Hand football to the left end coming behind you. Carry out your fake around end.

Coaching Points:

Left Halfback and Fullback—These men must go hard towards the defensive end. The left halfback gets first shot at him but the fullback gives help if it is needed. If none is needed, the fullback picks up any other defender in the area. They should use aggressive blocks rather than dropback-style blocks.

Left and Right Guards—The left and right guards should give the impression of leading a quarterback roll-out play by opening with the left foot. Then they should pivot on the second step (right foot) and turn back in the opposite direction. The right guard will probably block the defensive end as he crosses the line of scrimmage. The left guard should pick up any defensive player who crosses the line of scrimmage and poses a threat to the passer.

Wingback—The wingback must release downfield as quickly as possible without drawing attention to himself. He should make it appear that he is going downfield to block. He then looks for an opening in the deep right corner, and once he has it, turns on the speed.

Left End—The left end must be careful that he does not run into the left halfback, fullback, or quarterback as he prepares to take the handoff. Once he has the football, he places it under his arm as if running a simple reverse. How long he keeps the football under his arm before taking it out and throwing the pass will depend on the amount of pressure put on him by the defensive players. The left end must be sure to have a little depth as he sets up to throw. He should not get too close to the line of scrimmage where the pass might be batted down by a defensive lineman. Remember he has the option to run if the receiver is not open or if the defensive end is blocked and his path is clear to gain good yardage.

Right End—The right end's job is very important. He must attract the attention of the corner linebacker (or safety man) covering him. By running a short route and forcing this man to cover him, he will eliminate one potential defender in the deep area where the pass will be thrown.

Play 23

Flanker Reverse Pass

Basic Strategy:

The *Flanker Reverse Pass* is an outstanding reverse pass play that develops from the basic "I" formation off-tackle series. It is a relatively easy play to execute. All that is needed is an offensive team that likes to run off-tackle, a flanker who can throw the football, and a tight end who can decoy his way across the field and behind the secondary defense.

The play starts with a fake by the quarterback to the tailback driving into the off-tackle hole. This attracts the defensive linemen and linebackers to that area and should cause a quick rotation in the secondary. The flanker sprints behind the quarterback-tailback mesh point and takes a pitch from the quarterback. The flanker should be approximately six to eight yards deeper than the quarterback. He then looks downfield for the right end who has decoyed across field behind the defensive halfback.

Play Diagram:

Figure 23-1 shows how the *Flanker Reverse Pass* works.

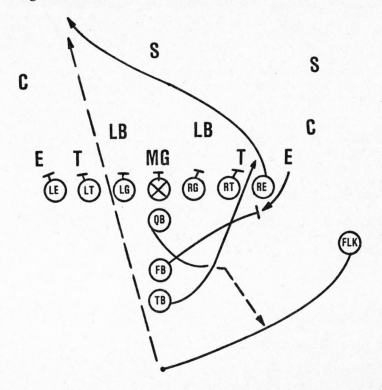

Figure 23-1 *Flanker Reverse Pass*

When to Use It:

● Use this play after the off-tackle running play has been established.

● Use the play if a flanker with passing ability is available.

(*Note*: A substitute quarterback could be inserted at the flanker position if the regular flanker cannot pass well.)

● Use the play against a defensive team that reacts quickly to the off-tackle play.

● This is a good play against inexperienced defensive backs.

● The play can be used inside the opponent's 10-yard line if other plays have failed to score.

● Weather should not affect this play more than any normal passing play.

● This play can be particularly effective if the offensive backs do a good job of faking the off-tackle play.

● The play can be run against any defense.

● Call this play in a short yardage situation as well as long yardage situations. The defensive backs will be looking for the running play more often than the long pass.

● Use the play if the regular passing quarterback is not in the game and the defensive backs are not anticipating a pass.

● This play is a good call against a stronger opponent and might supply an easy touchdown that is difficult to overcome.

When Not to Use It:

● This play is not a good call against a defensive team that stays in its pass defensive zones until the football has crossed the line of scrimmage.

● Do not use the play unless the flanker has some ability to pass the football.

● This play is not a good call inside your own five-yard line because much of the ball handling would have to take place inside the end zone area.

● The play might not be successful against a strong man-to-man pass coverage team whose backs are not easily fooled.

● Do not run the play until the off-tackle play has been established.

Position Assignments:

Flanker Reverse Pass versus 5-4 Defense

LE—Block defensive end.

LT—Block defensive tackle.

LG—Check firing linebacker. If none, help tackle, center or end if help is needed.

C—Block middle guard.

RG—Check linebacker. If he doesn't fire, help tackle, center, or end if help is needed.

RT—Block defensive tackle.

RE—Release towards far defensive back as if to make a downfield block. Slide past him, going deep for a pass from the flanker.

FB—Block defensive end.

TB—Fake a running play off-tackle as if you have the football.

QB—Fake a handoff to the tailback and immediately make pitch back to the flanker. After making the pitch, block any defensive player who threatens the flanker as he sets to pass.

Flanker—On the snap, sprint to a depth of six to eight yards behind the quarterback. Take the pitch and look for the right end dragging deep to the left side of the field. Pass as soon as he breaks behind the defensive back.

Coaching Points:

Right End—After releasing from the line of scrimmage, the right end heads for the defensive back on the far side of the field. He should start toward him in the same manner as if he were to make a downfield block on him. The right end should watch him carefully to detect the moment that he takes his eyes off him and concentrates on the fake off-tackle play. Once he does this, the right end must sprint past him and head for the end zone. He should be sure not to run past him too quickly or the defensive back will notice and cover him.

Flanker—It is very important that the flanker get proper distance from the tight end on his side so that he will arrive behind the quarterback just after the quarterback has completed his fake to the tailback (see Figures 23-2a, b & c). If the fake is made and he is not in position to receive the quarterback's pitch, the play timing is disrupted. Once the flanker has the football he may need to step back several steps as this will give him plenty of time to release the pass without pressure from the defenders.

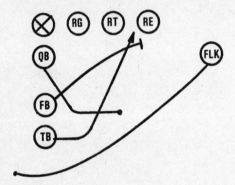

Figure 23-2a *INCORRECT. Flanker is too close in and has overrun the quarterback's pitch point.*

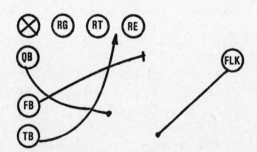

Figure 23-2b *INCORRECT. Flanker is too far out and has not yet reached the quarterback's pitch point.*

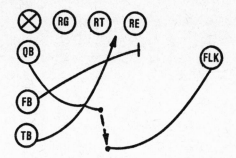

Figure 23-2c   *CORRECT. Flanker arrives behind quarter-*
back just after the QB has made a fake to
the tailback.

Quarterback—A good fake to the tailback is absolutely necessary for the play to be successful. Once this has been done, the
quarterback makes a one-handed pitch to the flanker, using the
same pitch motion he does on an option play. If, for some reason,
the flanker has not arrived at the pitch point after he has made the
fake to the tailback, the quarterback should continue parallel to the
line of scrimmage until the flanker is met (see Figure 23-3). Once
he has pitched the football, he shouldn't just stand and watch but
should block any defender in the area.

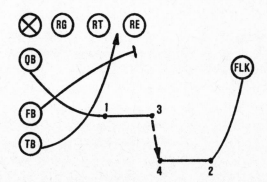

Figure 23-3   *The quarterback would like to pitch at point*
#1, but, since the flanker is only as far as
point #2, the QB must continue parallel to the
line of scrimmage until he arrives at point #3
and the flanker is at point #4 so the pitch can
be made.

Play 24

Quick Pitch Pass

Basic Strategy:

The *Quick Pitch Pass* is a quick striking pass play that is especially good in short yardage situations and inside the opponent's five-yard line. It is a play that must be executed quickly and with confidence. The passer will have little time to waste. He must receive the quick pitch from the quarterback and prepare to throw, all within a few steps. The left end must release quickly and not get delayed at the line of scrimmage. A quick judgment must be made by the left halfback as soon as he receives the pitch. He must decide whether he could gain more ground by tossing the pass to the end or by running to the outside. Hesitation in making this decision can cause the play to fail.

Play Diagram:

Figure 24-1 illustrates the *Quick Pitch Pass* against a 5-4 defense. A split backfield is used for illustration, but most any style backfield alignment is all right as long as a left halfback is available.

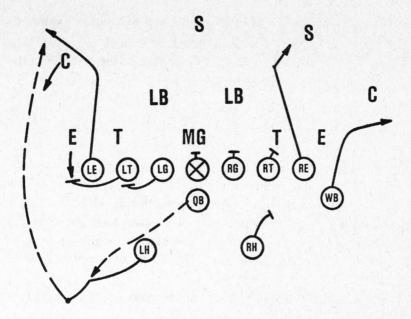

Figure 24-1 *Quick Pitch Pass*

When to Use It:

● This is an excellent short yardage play. Since the defensive backs will be playing closer to the line of scrimmage than usual, the left end will have a better chance to get behind them.

● This is a good play to run near the opposing team's goal line for the same reason as described in the previous entry.

● Use the play when a good athlete with passing ability is available for the left halfback position.

● The play works well against a team which does not delay the tight end when he releases for a pass.

● Use the play after the quick pitch play has been run several times.

● The play will be successful against defensive backs who come up quickly on apparent running plays.

● Call the play if the defensive end has not put a great deal of pressure on the left halfback on previous quick pitch plays.

● The play can work against most any defensive alignment.

● If the offensive team is noted for its quick pitch play, the *Quick Pitch Pass* would be a good call to make on the first play of the game.

When Not to Use It:

● Bad weather could affect the play, but this involves a judgment by you as to whether or not to use it. If the offensive team is trailing late in the game, it would be worth the risk.

● The play will have difficulty being successful if the defense is holding up the tight end on the line of scrimmage and delaying him from releasing on pass routes. (On this particular play the tight end *must* be able to release quickly.)

● Do not call the play if no passing halfback is available.

● This play may not be successful against a prevent defense.

● The play may not work well against a strong man-to-man defense where the tight end will be covered closely by a defensive back.

Position Assignments:

Quick Pitch Pass
versus 5-4 Defensive Alignment

LE—Release quickly. Look for the defensive back's movement. If he comes up fast toward the left halfback, sprint past him on a short down-and-out route. If he does not come up fast, turn in front of him and catch the pass in this area.

LT—Pull and block the first man outside the tight end.

LG—Pull and block first man to the outside.

C—Block middle guard.

RG—Check linebacker.

RT—Block defensive tackle.

(*Note*: Some coaches may prefer the center, right guard, and right tackle to *seal* the area to their left. This means the center would step to his left, checking the linebacker in case he fires, the right guard would cut off the middle guard, and the right tackle would check the linebacker on his side and block him if he fires.)

RE—Release towards safety in middle of field then try to get him to cover as you turn outside.

WB—Release to outside, forcing the outside linebacker to cover.

RHB—Block any defender to show on the right side.

QB—Step with the left foot towards the left halfback and toss the football to him.

LHB—Take the football as if running the quick pitch play. Stop suddenly and throw a pass to the left end.

Coaching Points:

Left Halfback—Properly catching the quick pitch from the quarterback should be worked on each day. On the snap of the football, the left halfback should step with the left foot at a 45-degree angle backwards to get depth. He must turn his body so that the quarterback can clearly see the numbers on the front of his jersey. He must also keep his hands and arms outstretched, ready to cradle the football as the quarterback tosses it to him. (*Note*: This body position will provide the quarterback with a good target area—the outstretched arms and chest area. The left halfback must never force the quarterback to have to make the toss to a back sprinting full speed away from him with no "target area" to toss the football into.) Once he has caught the football from the quarterback, the left halfback must evaluate his situation. He must ask himself, "Do I have running room?" "Has the tight end been delayed at the line of scrimmage?" "Is the tight end behind the secondary defender?" At this point, he must make a quick judgment whether to pass or run.

Play 25

Bounce Pass, Double Pass

Basic Strategy:

The *Bounce Pass, Double Pass* is a dangerous surprise play that should be used only after it has been practiced for a considerable length of time. It should be called only after you have given the situation serious consideration. However, if practiced often and if the players have confidence in it, the play could result in a sure touchdown.

To the defensive players, this play seems to be nothing more than a poorly thrown pass to the flanker since the football is thrown into the ground several yards away from the flanker. But because the pass is thrown backward (away from the line of scrimmage) it is actually a lateral rather than a pass and is still a live ball. The flanker must pretend to relax and casually reach down and pick up the football. Hopefully, the defensive players will relax, thinking the play is over. Meanwhile, the left end sprints toward the safety man on his side of the defense, as if to make a downfield block. (*Note*: Some coaches may prefer the left end to actually execute a downfield block on the safety man.) Then suddenly, the left end sprints deep to the right side getting behind the safety men on that side. By that time, the flanker has picked up the football and fires a long pass to the left end, who should be all alone in the secondary.

The key to the success of this play is the ability of the offensive players to appear to relax after the football hits the ground, thereby causing the defensive players to relax also.

Play Diagram:

This unusual play is diagrammed in Figure 25-1. The two running backs are in an "I" formation here, but can be placed in any arrangement. The play is illustrated against a 6-2 defensive alignment.

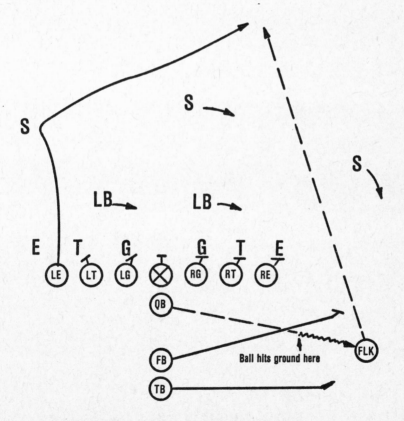

Figure 25-1 *Bounce Pass, Double Pass*

When to Use It:

● Because of the difficulty in executing this play, it should probably be used only in emergency situations when the offensive team is desperate to score.

● Call this play on first down or on second down and short yardage. By doing so, if the play fails to work or the football bounces out-of-bounds, the offensive team will still have opportunities to make the next first down.

● Since this play will probably go all the way for a touchdown or fail completely, it is a good call on very long yardage situations.

● It is a good call at the end of the first half or at the end of the game.

● It is a good call against a very strong defensive opponent who is not allowing your offense many first downs, much less a score.

● It is a good call against inexperienced defensive backs.

● Call the play against aggressive defensive backs who come up quickly.

● The play probably works best against a zone-type defensive secondary.

● Use the play if the flanker is a good long passer.

● The play can be used effectively against any defense.

When Not to Use It:

● Do not use the play if your team is ahead in a tight game.

● Do not use the play until it has been practiced many times.

● Bad weather will have some effect on this play.

● Do not use the play near the offensive team's goal line. The bounce pass to the flanker might be recovered by a defender in the end zone or near the goal line.

● Do not use the play if the flanker does not have a strong arm to throw the long pass.

● The play might not work as well against a man-to-man defense where the left end will be covered closely all over the field.

● Because of the limited area of the field for the left end to run his route, the play may not work well near the opponent's goal line. (*Example*: If the football is on the opponent's six-yard line there is not enough room for the left end to run his route.)

Position Assignments:

Bounce Pass, Double Pass versus 6-2 Defense

LE—Release downfield toward safety man on your side. Sprint past him (or fake downfield block on him) and head for deep right side of the defense. Look for pass from flanker.

LT—Block defensive tackle.

LG—Block defensive guard.

C—Check firing linebacker or help either guard with the defensive guard.

RG—Block defensive guard.

RT—Block defensive tackle.

RE—Block defensive end (be sure to stay with him as long as possible).

QB—Take snap and immediately fire pass to flanker, throwing the football so that it will hit the ground several yards before it gets to the flanker.

FB—Sprint to an area in *front* of the flanker and block any defender to show.

TB—Sprint to an area *behind* the flanker to offer help in case the football is not recovered by the flanker. (*Example*: Should a defender get to the football before the flanker picks it up, the tailback is in position to tackle the defender.)

Flanker—Line up several yards off the line of scrimmage. Turn towards the quarterback as he throws the bounce pass. Get between the football and the sideline as the ball is coming toward you. After the football has hit the ground and bounced several times, pick it up casually. Look at the defenders. If they have relaxed, thinking the ball is dead, continue to "fake" for another second or two, then pass to the left end downfield. If the defenders are not fooled, either pass quickly to the left end or run with the football.

Coaching Points:

All Players—All players must remember that the bounce pass to the flanker is a live ball and can be picked up and advanced by a defensive player. They must be alert to this possibility!

Flanker—Of course, the flanker is the key to the success of this play. If he appears too anxious to get to the football after it has hit the ground he will give away the surprise of the play. He must have control of himself as he picks up the football. If a defender realizes the football is a live ball and attempts to pick it up, he must get to the ball before the defender does. Once he is ready to pass he must do it quickly. The flanker should look upfield and fire the pass, checking only to be sure several defensive backs haven't read the play and covered the receiver.

Right End—The right end must stay with his defensive end and block him until the play is completely over, or at least until the flanker has passed the football. The defensive end is the player who is most likely to recognize the bounce pass for what it is—a live ball. The right end's block will keep him from reacting to the football before the flanker has a chance to complete his play.

Quarterback—The quarterback must practice throwing the bounce pass many times to get the feel of how hard to throw it, how far to throw it and so on. Generally speaking, the softer the pass is thrown, the easier it will be to catch after it has hit the ground.

Fullback—The fullback's job is to offer general protection to the flanker to give him time to do his job. He should block the first defender to threaten the flanker and stay with his block on this player until the pass has been thrown to the left end.

Tailback—The tailback has two responsibilities. One is to recover the football if the flanker cannot handle the bounce pass for any reason. Second, it is his job to tackle any defender who might pick up the football and attempt to score.

Play 26

Double Reverse Pass

Basic Strategy:

The *Double Reverse Pass* is a razzle-dazzle play that attracts the attention of the defense to the offensive backfield area, allowing the fullback to slip unnoticed down the sidelines for a pass. It is not a difficult play to execute, despite the fact that it may appear complicated.

The play begins as a sweep to the right side. The backfield flow immediately draws the defensive players in position to stop the sweep. The halfback running the sweep then hands off to the slotback for an apparent reverse play. The slotback then tosses the football back to the quarterback who has moved to a position about ten yards behind the line of scrimmage. By this time, the fullback has sprinted outside the secondary defenders and down the right sideline and will receive a pass from the quarterback.

This is an excellent play because all offensive teams have some type of sweep play plus a reverse that originates from the sweep. It is a highly deceptive play that players enjoy using.

Play Diagram:

The *Double Reverse Pass* is shown in Figure 26-1. It can also be executed by a wingback and tight end rather than a slotback and split end (tight end goes down and across deep and the wingback runs the reverse).

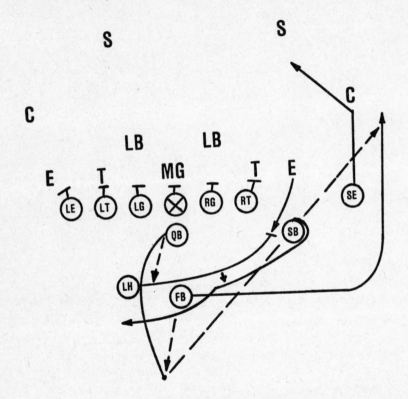

Figure 26-1   *Double Reverse Pass*

When to Use It:

- Run this play after the sweep has been successful.
- Run the play after the reverse by the slotback has been shown.

● Use the play against a defensive unit that reacts quickly to the flow of a running play.

● Use the play against a man-to-man pass defense which may fail to assign a defensive player to cover the offensive fullback.

● Use the play against a weak or inexperienced defensive secondary.

● This is a good play for a team with good ball handlers and fakers in the offensive backfield.

● Use the play if the fullback is a good pass receiver.

● This is a good short yardage play, since the defensive players will be close to the line of scrimmage (secondary included), and the fullback may find it easy to get open down the sidelines.

● This is a good play to use at any time, but especially near the end of the first half and at the end of the game.

● The play works well against any defense.

● Use the play often to the wide side of the field as this will allow the fullback plenty of room to get open.

When Not to Use It:

● Bad weather may affect the use of this play since the football must be handled by the quarterback, halfback, slotback, quarterback again and then by the fullback catching the pass.

● The coach should use judgment in calling this play inside his own 10-yard line. Because of the ball handling involved, there is the risk of a fumble.

● The play may have difficulty against a defensive team that plays man-to-man defense and has a good defender assigned to cover the fullback wherever he goes.

● Do not try this play if the running backs (halfback and slotback) are not good ball handlers, as each will be required to take and make a handoff.

● It is our feeling that the play is not a good call inside the opponent's five-yard line. If not run properly, the play could loose yardage (halfback, slotback, or quarterback tackled behind line of scrimmage) and we do not feel we can afford to lose any yardage in this critical area.

Position Assignments:

Double Reverse Pass versus 5-4 Defense

LE—Block defensive end.

LT—Block defensive tackle.

LG—Check firing linebacker. If none, help with middle guard or defensive tackle.

C—Block middle guard.

RG—Check firing linebacker. If none, help with middle guard or defensive tackle.

RT—Block defensive tackle.

Split End—Release straight ahead for eight yards then cut to the deep middle.

QB—Make toss to left halfback as on normal sweep. Drop to depth of 10 yards. Take pitch from slotback. Throw to fullback swinging down the sideline.

LHB—After taking football from quarterback start on sweep route to the right. Hand football to slotback coming behind you. Block defensive end.

Slotback—Open to the outside and come behind the left halfback. Take a handoff as on a reverse. After running several steps toss football to quarterback and continue running reverse route.

FB—Sprint to the right as if leading a sweep play. Continue outside the defense and turn upfield looking for the pass from the quarterback.

Coaching Points:

Fullback—As the fullback gets outside the defensive end's area he may wish to slow down slightly and maybe even look back toward the slotback as he makes his fake reverse. This should tend to cause any defensive player who may be watching him to feel sure he is no longer a factor in the play. Once the defenders have taken their eyes off him he should sprint hard upfield and be ready to receive the pass from the quarterback.

Left Halfback—The left halfback has three important duties: faking the sweep, handing the football to the slotback and blocking the defensive end. He must be sure to get plenty of practice handing the football off to the slotback properly. Also, he should be sure to make a good block on the defensive end.

Slotback—The slotback should get plenty of practice making the toss back to the quarterback. He must be sure to continue faking once he has made the pitch.

Split End—The split end must draw as much attention to himself as possible, opening the deep right area for the fullback's route.

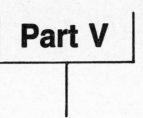

Part V

Developing Surprise Plays for Kicking Situations

Since this entire section deals with using surprise plays in *kicking* situations there is one point that should be stressed. It is probably more dangerous to call a surprise play in a kicking situation than in a normal situation. If a surprise play fails to work on first, second, or even third down there is still at least one more down to try another play or to punt the football. However, when a surprise play is tried in place of a punt the play *must* work or the football goes over to the opponent immediately. If a surprise play fails to work on an extra point attempt there is no second chance to try something different. There is *definitely* a place for surprise plays in the kicking game, but you are urged to use these plays wisely. Thought must be given to the score of the game, the field position, the time left in the game and the strength of the opponent. When sound judgment is used in calling surprise plays during kicking situations these special plays will often turn the complexion of the game to the user's favor.

Play 27

Fake Punt, Pass to the Tight End

Basic Strategy:

The simple strategy of the *Fake Punt, Pass to the Tight End* is to give every appearance of making a normal punt, but instead have the punter throw a short pass to one of the tight ends. This play is designed primarily as a first down play and is planned to make just enough yardage to keep possession of the football. However, it is very likely to turn into a long gainer.

The offensive team lines up in normal punt formation. This formation can vary slightly depending on the preference of the coach, but must contain two tight ends. The reason for having two tight ends is to give the passer the option of throwing to his right or his left depending on which end is more open.

The football is snapped to the punter, who catches the ball and starts his normal kicking steps. This is to convince the defense that

a punt, as usual, is about to be made. On the second step the
punter stops his punting motion, cocks his arm, and fires a pass to
one of the tight ends. Every precaution should be taken to make
the play look like a normal punt except that the offensive linemen
cannot go downfield as they would when covering a punt. The two
tight ends must know exactly how many yards are needed for a first
down and go several yards *beyond* that point before turning to the
outside for the pass. It would be tragic for a tight end to catch this
surprise pass only to find he has failed to gain the necessary first
down yardage by a few feet.

Play Diagram:

Figure 27-1 shows the *Fake Punt, Pass to the Tight End* play.
Almost any formation or positioning of players is all right as long as
there are two tight ends.

When to Use It:

- Use the play if the punter is a capable passer.
- Use the play if both tight ends are good short receivers.
- Use this play when it becomes necessary to make the first
down and keep the football in order to stay in the game.
- Use the play against a defensive team that is strong against
the normal run and pass offense.
- The play should work well against an inexperienced or
young defensive team.
- Call the play if the regular punter is injured and the back-up
punter is not adequate. (Insert the quarterback to run the play.)
- Use the play when the offensive team is across the 50-yard
line into the enemy territory (such as on the defense's 40-yard
line). If the play does not succeed, the team that tried the surprise
play will still be in good field position.
- Use the play when the defensive team ignores the ends as
they cover punts on normal punting situations.
- The play can work against almost any punt receiving formation.

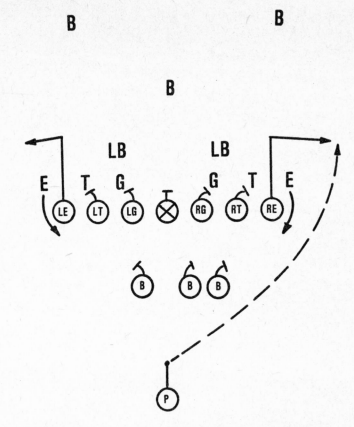

Figure 27-1 *Fake Punt, Pass to the Tight End*

• The play can be called at any point of the game, but should be saved until it is needed. There is no reason to show the play when ahead by 20 points.

When Not to Use It:

• Do not call the play if the punter is not capable of accurately throwing a short pass.

• If bad weather has affected other passes during the game this play might be considered a risk.

• Do not call this play if the defensive team assigns two defenders to cover the tight ends as they release on normal punt situations, as they might have difficulty getting open.

- The play must never be called inside the opponent's 30-yard line where a normal punt would not be expected to take place.

- Do not use the play against an outclassed opponent in order to run up the score.

Position Assignments:

LE—Release from the line of scrimmage. Go at least three yards beyond the distance needed for a first down. Turn sharply to the outside, angling slightly back toward the passer.

LT—Block first defender head-on or to the outside.

LG—Block first defender head-on or to the outside.

C—Block any defender head-on. If none, check for firing linebacker.

RG—Block first defender head-on or to the outside.

RT—Block first defender head-on or to the outside.

RE—Release from the line of scrimmage. Go at least three yards beyond the distance needed for a first down. Turn sharply to the outside, angling slightly back toward the passer.

Three Blocking Backs—Block first defenders to cross the line of scrimmage. Check first for defenders coming up the middle, then check to the outside.

Punter—Receive football and begin steps as if to punt. Stop and throw pass to one of the tight ends.

Coaching Points:

Tackles, Guards, Center, Blocking Backs—On a normal punt play these players block their men for one or two counts, then release them and sprint downfield to cover the punt. On this play they must stay with their defenders, blocking them until the play has ended. They cannot go downfield (except for the backs who are being used as blockers on this play) during passing situations any-way.

Punter-Passer—Before the football is snapped the punter looks at the defensive alignment to see if there are any defenders in the area where he plans to pass. He tries to determine who, if anyone, will cover the tight ends on their routes. After taking the snap, he goes through the first two steps of the punting motion, but stops before making the kick. (*Note*: A heavy rush of defenders may force the punter to not complete his entire punting motion. He may need to throw quickly if the rush is heavy.)

Tight Ends—As the tight ends approach the line of scrim-mage, they should look at the chains and down marker to deter-mine how much yardage is needed for the first down. It is impor-tant that they run at least three yards beyond the necessary first down yardage. This will allow the receiver to make his cut to the outside and angle back towards the passer. This helps free the receiver from the defensive back (see Figures 27-2a & b). It also allows room for the receiver to come back for the football (if it has been thrown short) and still make the first down yardage.

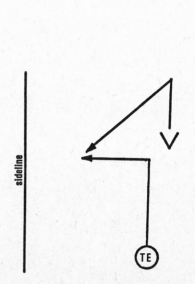

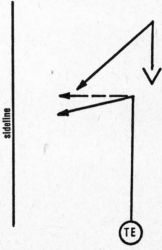

Figure 27-2a *Tight end runs 90° angle as he makes his cut. Defensive back has good chance to cover him.*

Figure 27-2b *Tight end cuts back toward passer. Defensive back has much tougher time breaking up this pass as he is farther away from re-ceiver.*

Play 28

Fake Punt and Run Inside

Basic Strategy:

The *Fake Punt and Run Inside* is an excellent short yardage fake-punt play. It is a good call when less than three yards are needed for the first down. Since there are many different and unusual punt receiving formations which a defensive team could use, a good scouting report is necessary in order to find a vulnerable area to attack. Once this spot has been found, use two blocking backs to double team in that area.

The center must work hard to develop an accurate short (five-yard) snap to the running back. The football must be snapped at a slight angle to the center's left. Also, the running back must get plenty of practice handling the snap from center. A fumble on the ball exchange from the center to the runner would not only ruin the play, but it could lose the game.

The "punter" must carry out his assignment well. He must, at all times, give the appearance of preparing to punt. All defensive personnel will have their eyes on him, and he must not alter his stance or steps in any way that might indicate that a surprise play is coming.

Play Diagram:

In Figure 28-1 the *Fake Punt and Run Inside* play is being run into the guard-tackle area on the right side of the offensive line. Remember that this play can be designed to run into any inside area where the defensive personnel may be weak.

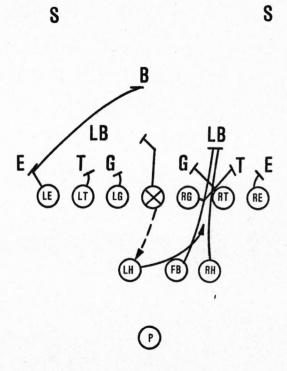

Figure 28-1 *Fake Punt and Run Inside*

When to Use It:

- Use the play on short yardage, fourth down situations.
- Use the play after finding the weakest defensive interior lineman on the punt receiving team.

• Call the play when it is vital that the offensive team keep possession of the football.

• Use the play when a strong runner is at one of the blocking back positions.

• Use the play against an opponent who replaces many regular defensive linemen with punt return specialists who are good at things like setting up return walls and so on, but are not strong enough to stop a power play inside.

• Use the play if the regular punter has been injured and the backup punter is not adequate.

• This is a good call if the offensive team's best offensive blockers remain in the lineup on punting situations.

• Call the play late in the first half or at the end of the game when time is running out. This can prevent a potential punt return for a touchdown by your opponent.

(*Note*: Be sure that you will not be left in poor field position with time on the clock if the play fails to get necessary first down yardage. *Example*: It would be all right to use the play near the 50-yard line, but not when backed up within your own 25-yard line. If the play failed inside your own 25, your opponent would need only a second or two on the clock to kick a field goal.)

• Call the play against an opponent who has a better than average punt return team.

• The play could be effective near the opponent's 35-yard line when a regular punt might not be a good call. If a punt is made, it will probably go into the end zone and be brought out to the 20-yard line, giving the kicking team very little net yardage on the play. Should the *Fake Punt and Run Inside* play fail, the opponent will still get the football inside their own 35-yard line. Therefore, the play is a pretty good risk in this area.

When Not to Use It:

• Rarely use the *Fake Punt and Run Inside* play inside your own 40-yard line. Should the play fail, you will be left in poor field position.

● Use the play only if a good power runner is at one of the blocking back positions.

● It may not be wise to call this play against a strong defensive team that leaves its regular defensive players in the game even on fourth down.

● Do not use the play when leading by a slight margin unless you are deep in your opponent's territory. If the play fails it could give a great boost in morale to your opponent.

Position Assignments:

Fake Punt and Run Inside versus a 6-2 Defense

LE—Bump defensive end and release on short safety back.

LT—Block defensive tackle.

LG—Block defensive guard.

C—Cut off linebacker on the weak side.

RG—Block defensive tackle by cross-blocking with right tackle.

RT—Block defensive guard by cross-blocking with right guard. (*Note*: Right tackle goes in *front* of the right guard and makes his block first. Right guard crosses *behind* right tackle to make his block.)

RE—Turn out on defensive end.

FB and RHB—Drive shoulder-to-shoulder towards the linebacker and double team block him. Drive him as far as possible off the line of scrimmage.

LHB—Take short snap from center and follow the double-team block of the fullback and right halfback.

Punter—Take normal stance 12-14 yards deep. After the ball has been snapped to the left halfback, check for a fumble or bad snap.

Coaching Points:

Runner and Blocking Backs—The runner and blocking backs should be sure to take their normal stance, just as they would if the punter was about to take the snap from center and kick the ball. They should not look at the hole where the play is about to be run. They should be lined up 4-5 yards off the line of scrimmage. The ball carrier must run straight and hard into the hole without getting too fancy or trying to get to the outside.

All Offensive Linemen—There are many ways the offensive linemen might be called on to block this play depending on the defense. *Wedge blocking* (three or more linemen driving shoulder-to-shoulder into a given area) is good for a play of this type, or simple one-on-one blocking can be used.

Play 29

Fake Punt and Run Wide

Basic Strategy:

The *Fake Punt and Run Wide* is designed primarily as a long
yardage play but can be equally effective when only short yardage
is needed. It works extremely well when the defense is trying to
block the kick, because the defensive linemen will be concentrating on rushing straight at the kicker and will not be too concerned
with covering against an outside run. The play is also very effective
against a team which likes to set up a return, especially if good
scouting reports indicate the probable direction of the return. Most
teams set up a punt return by having all defensive linemen, except
one, hit the offensive lineman in front of them and start in the
direction of the punt return wall. If the one defender who is coming across the line of scrimmage to check the punter can be eliminated, the ball carrier can run in the opposite direction of the punt
return wall (see Figure 29-2).

173

Play Diagrams:

Figure 29-1 shows the *Fake Punt and Run Wide* play against an eight-man front which is intent on rushing the punter and blocking the kick.

Figure 29-2 is an example of how the play can work against a team which is setting up a return wall.

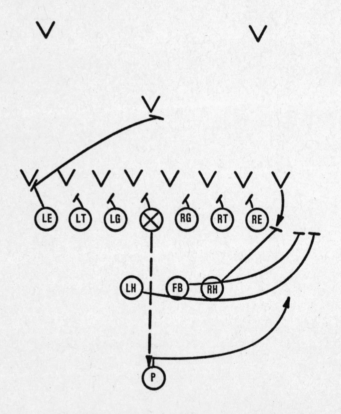

Figure 29-1 *Fake Punt and Run Wide. The defense is rushing eight men in an attempt to block the kick. We have good blocking angles on all defensive players who could stop the play.*

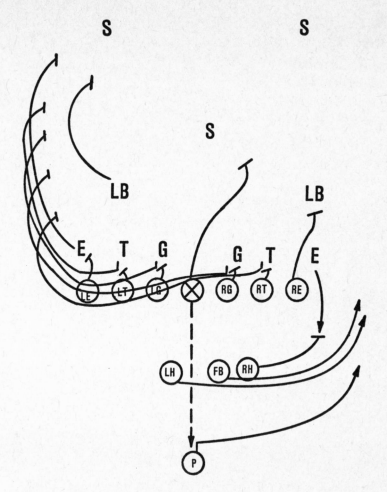

Figure 29-2 *Fake Punt and Run Wide. Defense is setting up a punt return wall. This gives good blocking angles as we run wide to the opposite side.*

When to Use It:

• Use the play to the wide side of the field when the ball is on the hash mark.

- Use the play to the short side of the field if the opposing team always sets up a punt return toward the wide side.

- Use the play when more than three yards are needed for a first down.

- This is a good call if the punter has good speed to get outside.

- Run this play against a weak defensive end.

- Use the play when it is absolutely necessary to keep possession of the football.

- Call the play against teams that substitute special players (such as fast linemen to set up a return wall) in place of regular defensive players.

- Use the play if good blockers are available at the three blocking back positions.

- Call the play as time is running out at the end of the half or at the end of the game (if it is needed then).

- Use the play against a team that specializes in good punt returns.

- Use the play if your offensive team has been moving the ball well, but a fumble or penalty has hurt your first down chances.

When Not to Use It:

- Do not use the play if the punter is a slow runner or if the defense would notice a change in punting personnel.

- Do not use the play until the offensive team nears the mid-field area. Should the play be used, and fail, inside the offensive team's 35-yard line it could lead to an easy score for the opposition.

- The play may have difficulty being run against a strong, experienced defensive end who plays his position well.

- Do not risk the play when ahead by a slight margin late in the game.

Position Assignments:

**Fake Punt and Run Wide
Against an Eight-Man Front That Is
Rushing the Kicker (Figure 29-1)**

LE—Block first player on your left for one count. Release and block the middle (short) safety man.

LT, LG, C, RG, RT, and RE—All block first man on your left side.

RHB—Block defensive end. Take him to the inside or outside depending on his angle of rush.

FB—Block first defender to show outside the defensive end.

LHB—Block second defender to show outside the defensive end.

Punter—Take snap and begin steps as if to punt. Sprint quickly to the outside behind the three blocking backs.

**Fake Punt and Run Wide
Against a Defense That Is Setting
Up a Punt Return (Figure 29-2)**

LE, LT, LG, RG, and RT—Block the defensive men over you, allowing them to release and form their punt return wall as they have been coached to do. Your block on these players should last for one count. The sooner the defensive players release to set up their wall, the less chance they will have of seeing the fake punt and run.

C—Release on middle (short) safety.

RE—Release and block linebacker your side.

RHB—Block defensive end, taking him inside or outside depending on the angle of his rush.

FB—Block first defender to show outside the defensive end.

LHB—Block second defender to show outside the defensive end.

Punter—Take snap and begin steps as if to punt. Sprint quickly to the outside behind the three blocking backs.

Coaching Points:

The key block of this play is the block on the defensive end toward the side where the play is being run. The best of the three blocking backs should be placed at the right halfback position so that he will be making this block.

The punter (ball carrier) must sprint as fast as he can to the outside as he begins his run. He should be a good open field runner who is capable of avoiding a tackler and getting the first down yardage.

Play 30

Fake Punt Reverse

Basic Strategy:

The *Fake Punt Reverse* is one of football's oldest, but rarely used, surprise plays and can be quite deceptive if the timing between several of the players is good. The football is snapped to the punter, who executes every kicking movement except actually kicking the ball. As the punter extends his right foot (for a right-footed kicker) to kick the ball he simultaneously extends his right arm (with the football in his right hand) behind him. The wingback comes behind the punter, takes the football out of his hand, and sprints around left end. This play can come as a complete surprise to defenders who are watching only the punter, and are rushing him hard in an effort to block the punt.

Be sure a great deal of work is done on the timing between the punter and the wingback. The wingback must be in position to take the football immediately after the punter places it behind him. The wingback must be careful to line up the same distance from the punter each time so that the carefully worked out timing will not be disturbed.

Play Diagram:

Figure 30-1 shows how the *Fake Punt Reverse* is set up. Figure 30-2 illustrates how the punter will look as he places the football behind him, ready to be taken by the wingback.

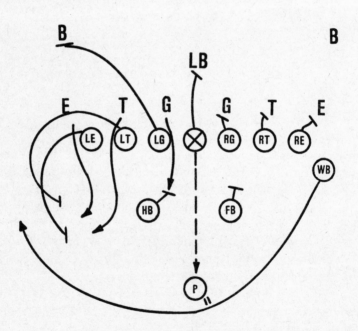

Figure 30-1 *Fake Punt Reverse*

Figure 30-2

When to Use It:

● This is an excellent play for a wingback with good speed.

● Use the play toward the young or inexperienced side of a defensive line.

● Use the play if the punter is less than adequate in his kicking yardage.

● Use the play against a strong defensive team that is not allowing many first downs (rushing or passing) when normal offensive plays are used.

● Use the play against a defensive team that returns punts well or is good at blocking punts.

● Use the play when the end and tackle on the side where the reverse is to be run are good blockers.

● Call the play late in the first half or late in the game as needed.

● This play can be very effective inside your opponent's 40-yard line.

When Not to Use It:

● This play can lose a great deal of yardage if not executed well. It may be a risk to use it inside your own 35-yard line.

● Do not use the play if ahead by a slight margin. Kick the football and put the pressure on the opposition to score.

● Use the play only if the wingback has good speed.

Position Assignments:

Fake Punt Reverse Against
a Six-Man Front
Punt Receiving Formation

LE—Release to the outside. Curl back several yards and block any defensive player who has seen the reverse and started after the wingback.

LT—Release to the outside, following the left end. Curl back several yards and block any defensive player who has seen the reverse and started after the wingback.

LG—Release and block the nearest defensive back on the side of the reverse.

C—Block middle linebacker.

RG—Block defensive guard.

RT—Block defensive tackle.

RE—Block defensive end.

HB—Block defensive guard on your side as he fires through.

FB—Block any defensive player who might break through on your side.

Punter—Step through entire kicking motion, but hand football to wingback with the right hand (extended behind you) just as the right foot (kicking foot) goes through the kicking motion.

WB—Sprint full speed behind the punter, taking the football out of his hand. Head for the outside, getting behind the blocks of the left end and left tackle.

Coaching Points:

Punter and Wingback—The punter and wingback can work on your timing without the rest of the players. This can be done during the off-season or after practice. Using a center will help perfect the timing.

Right Guard, Right Tackle, and Right End—These men must hold their blocks for the entire play. The play will take several seconds to develop, and the defensive players on the offensive right side must not be allowed to pursue the ball carrier after he takes the football from the punter.

Play 31

Fake Punt, Screen Pass
to the Halfback or End

Note: The *Fake Punt, Screen Pass to the Halfback or End* can be run using the left halfback or the left end as the pass receiver. If the end is used, he simply blocks the defensive end for one count, drops back behind the screen blockers, and receives the pass from the punter. For the purpose of explanation, we shall describe the play using the left halfback as the pass receiver.

Basic Strategy:

A screen pass, run from a regular formation, is one of the best plays in football. Many defensive teams are not well coached to defend against a screen pass. Even those that are often have a hard time reading the screen play. Most defensive players would never expect a screen pass during a fourth down punting situation. They are too concerned with rushing the punter or setting up a return wall to consider the possibility of a screen pass. So, the possibility of completing the *Fake Punt, Screen Pass to the Halfback* is very good.

There is very little difference in execution between this play and a regular screen pass from the offensive playbook. The backfield alignment will be different, of course. The screen pass can be to any of the three blocking backs. All that is needed for this play is a punter who can throw a short pass and a blocking back who can catch it. The offensive line should already know the fundamentals of blocking for a screen play and how to set up to the outside, ready to lead the ball carrier.

Play Diagram:

Figure 31-1 illustrates the *Fake Punt, Screen Pass to the Halfback*.

When to Use It:

● Use this play against a defense that rushes hard in an effort to block the punt.

● Use the play to the side of an inexperienced or young defensive end.

● This is a good play to use inside the opponent's 50-yard line.

● This play may be a better risk than punting to a team noted for its punt returns.

● Use the play late in the half or at the end of the game. If it fails to work, there should not be much time for the opposition to take advantage of the failure and score for themselves.

● Call the play if the defensive regulars have been removed in favor of punt return specialists who are not as good as the regulars in defending against passes and runs.

● Use the play when your punter is inadequate.

● This is an excellent play if one of the blocking backs is a good open field runner.

● Call the play if your offensive linemen are good at blocking for a screen pass.

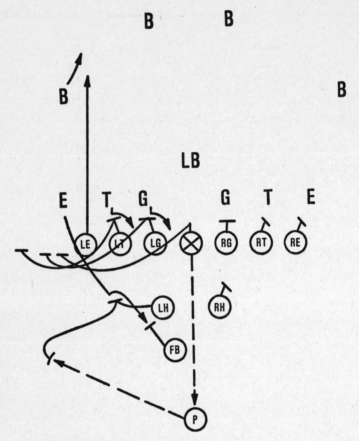

Figure 31-1 *Fake Punt, Screen Pass to the Halfback*

When Not to Use It:

● Your opponent will have good field position if you try this play inside your own 50-yard line and the play fails.

● Do not use the play if the punter is not an adequate short passer.

● Do not run this play against an experienced defensive end who is known to read the screen plays well.

● Avoid using the play when ahead by a slight margin.

Position Assignments:

Fake Punt, Screen Pass to the Halfback

LE—Release carrying nearest defensive back deep.

LT—Block defensive tackle two counts; release and set up screen to the outside.

LG—Block defensive guard two counts (1001, 1002); release and set up screen to the outside.

C—Check for firing linebacker. If none, hold up two counts; release and set up screen to the outside.

RG—Block defensive guard.

RT—Block defensive tackle.

RE—Block defensive end.

LHB—Meet and block defensive end for one good count. Force him to release inside you, and then set up behind screen blockers, looking for the pass from the punter. As you receive the pass, yell "Go" to the screen blockers.

RHB—Block the first defender who crosses the line of scrimmage in your area.

FB—Block the defensive end on your side after the left halfback has released him.

Punter—Take the snap from center and start your punting steps. Stop and fire screen pass to the left halfback.

Coaching Points:

Punter-Passer—If the defensive end reads the screen and goes with the left halfback, the punter-passer should run directly at the defensive end. If the end comes up to take him, he should drop a short pass over the end's head to the left halfback. If the end continues to cover the halfback, the punter-passer should run the football.

Left Halfback—If the defensive end covers the left halfback as he sets up in position to catch the pass, the halfback should start sprinting upfield. If the end leaves him and rushes the passer, the passer will drop a short pass over the end's head to the halfback. If the end covers him, the passer will run the football.

Play 32

Fake Extra Point
or Field Goal,
Pass to Halfback

Basic Strategy:

Before the *Fake Extra Point or Field Goal, Pass to Halfback* can be used, the kicking team must install a new type of huddle that is used prior to any extra point or field goal attempt. Instead of huddling directly behind the football, the huddle must be made about 10-12 yards to the right of the football and, of course, 6-8 yards from the line of scrimmage. This is not really an unusual type of huddle. Many teams do this in order to give the kicker space to set up his kicking tee and get himself prepared to kick.

The play is a simple one but takes a little work on timing. As soon as an extra point or field goal situation develops, the extra point/field goal team takes the field. The kicker starts placing his kicking tee in position (usually about seven yards behind the football), while the other ten team members form their huddle to the right of the football. The play is called in the huddle and the snapper (left end) and the holder leave the huddle. As soon as they are set in their positions the other eight players break huddle and sprint to the line of scrimmage, taking positions as shown later in the play diagram. As soon as the eight players have been set and still for one second on the line of scrimmage the football is snapped to the kicker, who immediately fires a pass to the halfback who is waiting behind a wall of blockers. The idea of this play, of course, is for the defensive players to become confused by the strange formation and fail to send enough (or any) defenders to the area where the halfback will receive the pass. Unless the defense sends at least six players to the area of the offensive linemen, they will have little chance to stop the play. Even if they send defensive players to the offensive line area, they probably won't line up in a well-balanced defensive alignment. What usually results is total defensive confusion. Some players will stay in their normal defensive positions, although there isn't an offensive player near them. Others will hurry to cover the new formation. Either action will probably result in an unsound defensive alignment.

Play Diagram:

Figure 32-1 shows the offensive huddle and the positions of all 11 players as they run *Fake Extra Point or Field Goal, Pass to the Halfback*.

When to Use It:

● Use this play when *two* points are needed instead of one on an extra point attempt.

● Use the play when a fake field goal attempt is desired.

● The play will almost always work against a young or inexperienced defensive team.

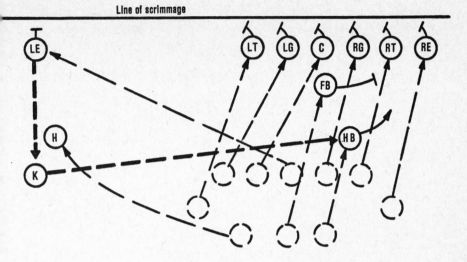

Figure 32-1 *Fake Extra Point or Field Goal, Pass to the Halfback. Kicker (K) gets kicking tee set while others huddle. Left end (LE) and holder (H) break huddle and take positions first. After they are set, other team members sprint to the line of scrimmage and quickly get set. Football is snapped to kicker, who fires a pass to the halfback. All this should take place before defense has time to adjust.*

● Call the play if the kicker can throw an accurate short pass.

● Use the play in a field goal situation against a strong opponent whose defense had not allowed much yardage rushing or passing when normal offensive plays had been used.

When Not to Use It:

● Do not use the play against a defensive team that is known to adjust quickly to unusual offensive formations.

● Do not show the play if the extra point kicker is good and two points are not needed to win the game or to go ahead of an opponent.

• Do not use the play if the field goal kicker is good, the football is in field goal range and more than three points are not needed to tie or go ahead of an opponent.

• Do not attempt the play if the kicker is not an adequate short passer.

Position Assignments:

LE—Break the huddle, line up over the football, and make a snap to the kicker. Block any defender over you.

LT—Sprint to the line of scrimmage, about ten yards from the left end (and the football). Block first defender to your inside.

LG—Sprint to the line of scrimmage and line up next to the left tackle. Block first defender to your inside.

C—Sprint to the line of scrimmage. Line up next to the left guard. Block first defender to your inside.

RG—Sprint to the line of scrimmage and line up next to the center. Block the first defender to your inside.

RT—Sprint to the line of scrimmage and line up next to the right guard. Block the first defender to your inside.

RE—Sprint to the line of scrimmage and line up next to the right tackle. Block the first defender to your inside.

Holder—Leave the huddle early with the left end. Take your position as if you were to take the snap from center and hold the football for an extra point or field goal attempt.

Kicker—Never go to the huddle. Place kicking tee in normal kicking position. Take snap from the left end and fire a short pass to the halfback.

FB—Sprint to the line of scrimmage and take a two-point stance behind the center (about three yards deep). Block any defender who gets near the pass receiver.

HB—Sprint to the line of scrimmage and take a position about five yards behind the right guard. Take pass from the kicker and run to daylight.

Coaching Points:

Interior Offensive Linemen—Remember, this is a pass play that develops quickly so it will be best for offensive linemen to use a two-point upright stance rather than getting into a three- or four-point stance.

Ends—The main job of the ends is to block on the line of scrimmage as they will not be needed downfield.

All Players—All players should keep in mind at all times that the play must be done quickly so that the defensive players will not have time to adjust to the new formation or to think to call a time out (which would kill the play). The kicker must call for the snap as soon as all players have been set for a second.

Play 33

Fake Extra Point
or Field Goal,
Pass to the Center

Special Note: Be sure you have read Play 32 before attempting the *Fake Extra Point or Field Goal, Pass to the Center.* This play is to be used after the defensive players have adjusted to the offensive strength of Play 32. The offensive strength of Play 32 is to the side that has six offensive linemen and two backs. Read again how to set **up** the play (kicker gets his kicking tee set, left end and holder break the huddle, then other eight team members take their positions). Once this has been done and there are only one or two defenders in the area of the left end (snapper), Play 33 is ready to be run.

194

Basic Strategy:

The idea of this play is to make it look like Play 32 (see previous section) is to be run again. Play 32 featured a pass from the kicker to the halfback. This play is also a pass play. The football is snapped to the holder. The kicker begins his steps and goes through his entire kicking motion as if kicking an extra point or field goal. The holder then picks up the football from the tee and fires a pass to the left end who has just snapped the football. There are two surprise points to this play. First, the defenders, seeing the unusual formation, will think the pass to the halfback (Play 32) is coming again. The second surprise is the pass to the left end, as most defenders will think of the left end as the snapper and disregard him as a pass receiver.

This play is an excellent example of how surprise plays force players, rather than coaches, to have to make sudden decisions and adjustments.

Play Diagram:

Figure 33-1 shows the operation of the *Fake Extra Point or Field Goal, Pass to the Center.* We have intentionally not placed any defensive players on the diagram because there is no way to determine how the defensive players will react to the formation. The main point to remember is that this play should not be called until it has been shown that most defensive players will leave the area near the snapper (left end) before the ball is snapped, leaving the left end plenty of room to get open for a pass.

When to Use It:

• Use this play in the same game that Play 32 was shown, or use it the week following the showing of Play 32 (these two plays complement each other).

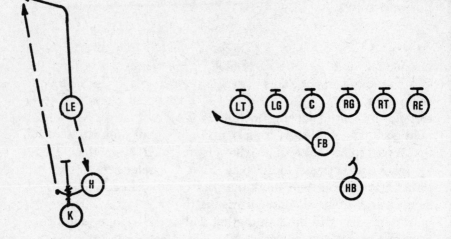

Figure 33-1 *Fake Extra Point or Field Goal, Pass to the Center*

● Use this play after defenders have shifted to the strong side of this unusual formation (the strong side is the side containing six offensive players on the line of scrimmage).

● Use the play if the holder is an adequate short passer.

● Use the play if the left end can make the snap to the holder and also catch a short pass well.

● Use this play if two points are needed rather than one point as would be gained by kicking.

● Use the play against inexperienced defensive players.

● This is a good play to use when slightly out of your field goal kicker's range (but the defense doesn't know it).

When Not to Use It:

● Do not call the play if the kicker is very accurate and only one point (extra point) or three points (field goal) is needed to win or go ahead in the score.

• Do not call the play until Play 32 has been shown.

• Do not show this play if far ahead or far behind in the score. Save it until it is needed to win a close game.

Position Assignments:

(*Note*: Refer to Play 32 to see how all players break the huddle and approach the line of scrimmage.)

LE—Snap football to the holder. Release for a pass, finding an open spot in the defensive secondary.

Holder—Take normal position as if to hold for a kick. Pick up football from the tee before it is kicked and fire short pass to the left end (snapper).

Kicker—Line up as if to kick. Go through all normal steps but do not kick the football. Block any defender who rushes the holder as he sets to pass.

LT, LG, C, RG, RT, RE, FB, HB—Be the last to break the huddle. Attract attention so that many defensive players will rush to your area. Once the ball has been snapped block any defender over you. Your main job on this play is to draw defensive players to your area and away from the *left end* area.

Coaching Points

Left End (Snapper)—Before the left end snaps the ball, he glances at the area in front of him and to each side. He should find the most open area to run his pass route. The *holder* should be doing the same thing in reference to looking for your most likely open spot.

Offensive Linemen—The linemen should remember that this is a pass play and that they are not allowed to go downfield. The play should develop so quickly and they should be so far from the action, that they will not figure prominently in the play. However, they must pass-block the defender in front of them to cut down any ideas of pursuit he might have.

Fullback—The fullback releases to the left of the left tackle as an alternate receiver, in case something detains the left end from getting open.

Halfback—The halfback turns toward the holder. He could be an alternate receiver in case the left end (or fullback) cannot get open.

Play 34

Fake Extra Point
or Field Goal
and Run

Basic Strategy:

There are two factors that help make the *Fake Extra Point or Field Goal and Run* a success: (1) The motion by the blocking back on the left side which provides an extra blocker in the area where the ball carrier is going. (Also, this sudden motion will be totally unexpected and may cause the defense to jump offsides.) (2) Most defensive teams, in extra point or field goal situations, place eight defensive men on the line of scrimmage with instructions to fire the gaps and block the kick. (Defensive linemen will rarely be head-on offensive linemen as this would not allow them to penetrate across the line of scrimmage as fast.) The defensive players firing the gaps will provide excellent blocking angles for the offensive linemen. The play has little deception as far as ball handling is concerned, but the good blocking angles, together with the surprise element, give the play good chance for success.

When all offensive players are set on the line of scrimmage the blocking back on the left side is sent in motion to the right. Just as he passes the center the football is snapped to the kicker. The kicker immediately heads for the outside behind the blocking of the holder, the blocking back in motion and the other eight offensive players, each of whom will have a blocking angle on a defender.

Play Diagram:

Figure 34-1 shows the *Fake Extra Point or Field Goal and Run* play. Reverse the blocking assignments and send the right blocking back in motion to the left to run the play to the other side.

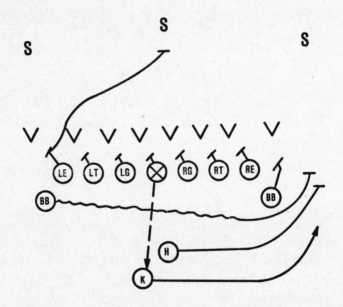

Figure 34-1   *Fake Extra Point or Field Goal and Run*

When to Use It:

- Use the play if two points instead of one are needed in an extra point situation.
- Use this play if six points, instead of three, are needed in a situation where a field goal or touchdown is within range.
- Call this play if the kicker has some speed with which to get outside.
- Use the play when the defensive players are in the gaps providing good blocking angles.
- The play can work well against inexperienced defensive players.
- Use the play against a defensive team whose regular defensive starters have been removed and replaced by defenders whose specialty is blocking kicks.
- This is a good call against slow defensive players.
- This play can be used in a field goal situation simply to make a first down.

When Not to Use It:

- Do not risk the play if one point is all that is needed on an extra point attempt to stay ahead of the opponent in the score.
- Do not risk the play if three points (field goal) are all that is needed to stay ahead of an opponent, and the kicker is in range.
- Do not use the play unless the kicker has a little ability to run the football or has a little speed.
- The play will have little chance to work against a defense that is spread out or that has strong outside coverage.
- Do not call the play, in a field goal situation, if the kicker is not in his range. The defensive players, if well coached, will know the kicker is not within range and will suspect some type of surprise play.

Position Assignments:

Fake Extra Point or Field Goal and Run
versus a Gap-8 Defense

LE—Block first defender to your left; release and go for middle safety man.

LT—Block first defender to your left.

LG—Block first defender to your left.

C—Block first defender to your left.

RG—Block first defender to your left.

RT—Block first defender to your left.

RE—Block first defender to your left.

Blocking Back on Right Side—Block first defender to your left.

Blocking Back on Left Side—Go in motion to the right. Block first defensive player to show.

Holder—Get in position to handle regular extra point or field goal snap from center. As ball is snapped to kicker, sprint to the right; block first defender to show.

Kicker—Take normal kicking stance. Receive football and sprint to the right following blocks of the holder, left blocking back in motion and other eight offensive players.

Coaching Points:

Left Blocking Back—The motion of the left blocking back should be at full speed. He should not give the defense time to react to his motion and shift any defensive players in the direction he is going. He must never pass up blocking the first defensive player he meets.

Holder—If the kicker is extremely slow with no running ability at all, let the football be snapped to the holder, who makes the run instead of the kicker.

Right Blocking Back—The right blocking back blocks the first defensive player to his left side. However, if that player attempts to rush to his outside (or if there is no player to his inside, but one is lined up to his outside), he blocks the defender to the outside and the left blocking back and holder will lead the ball carrier through the hole to his inside (see Figure 34-2).

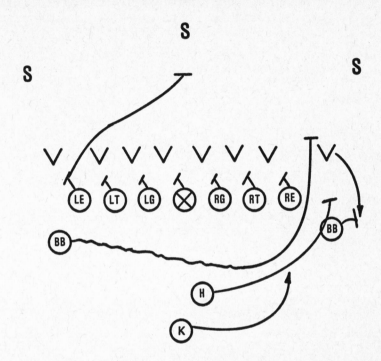

Figure 34-2 *Defensive end on the right side rushes out-side. Right blocking back blocks him to the outside and the left blocking back and holder lead the ball carrier through the hole to the inside.*

Center—The center should remember that the football is snapped to the kicker. He must try to hit him just above the belt with the football. He should not make the snap so hard that it will be difficult to handle. The kicker needs to be able to catch the ball easily and start his run immediately.

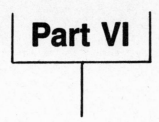

Part VI

Confusing the Defense
with Surprise Formations

The purpose of this section is to present surprise formations, shifts, and movements that will cause confusion among defensive players, forcing them to make adjustments which will disrupt the carefully planned balance of their defense. Defensive confusion causes a lack of confidence among players, causing their reactions to be slow and their movements to be unsure.

We will not use the same format or outline in this section as we have in the previous parts of the book. Instead, we will show, through a series of illustrations, how surprise formations, shifts and movements can be used to the advantage of the offense and how they can be incorporated into almost any offensive system.

Play 35

Quarterback Shift

The *Quarterback Shift* is so unusual that the first thing that will probably happen is an offsides penalty against an overly aggressive defensive player. In this case, a five-yard gain is already insured before the ball is even snapped. If the defense doesn't jump offsides, the quarterback's shift will place him in position to take advantage of the defense at some point. The only extra duty in installing this shift will be to teach the center to make a short snap to a back lined up several yards off the line of scrimmage and, at times, at a slight angle to the center. Following are some examples of how to use the *Quarterback Shift* to your advantage.

Figure 35-1 shows the quarterback shifting from his normal position under the center to a position five to seven yards deep and directly behind the center. This new position offers the quarterback a chance to throw a pass without first having to take a snap from center in the conventional method and drop back to a depth of five to seven yards. This shift to a shotgun style offense creates a whole new problem for the defense.

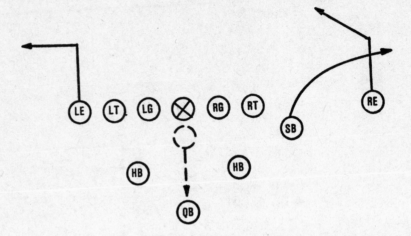

Figure 35-1 *Quarterback shifts to passing position, creating shotgun style offense.*

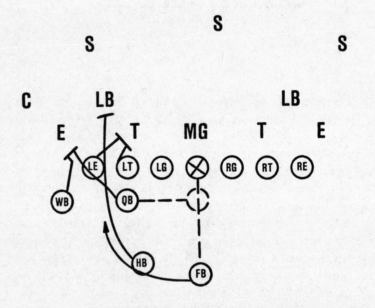

Figure 35-2 *Quarterback shifts to his left and helps wingback double team the defensive end on the 5-4 Eagle Defense. Ball is snapped to the fullback, who runs off tackle. QB used as a blocker here.*

In executing this shift, as with all examples shown here, the quarterback must first approach the center as if to take a normal snap, then quickly move to his new position and remain set for a second before the football is snapped.

Figure 35-2 illustrates a quarterback shift which creates excellent power play possibilities. In this diagram, the quarterback has shifted three to four yards to his left, placing himself in good position to double team the defensive end with the wingback on an off-tackle power play. So here the quarterback is used as a blocker.

The running ability of the quarterback is put to use in the play shown in Figure 35-3. By shifting to a halfback position, the quarterback can run a sweep play behind maximum blocking protection. (*Note*: The quarterback should cheat in toward the fullback to give the center an easier snap angle.)

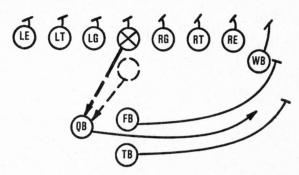

Figure 35-3 *Quarterback shifts to halfback and runs a sweep.*

Figure 35-4 shows the quarterback being used as a punter while Figure 35-5 illustrates the quarterback in position to quick kick.

As soon as it is decided that the *Quarterback Shift* will be used, begin working with the offensive center on his short snaps. Allow him to practice every day, making snaps to the fullback and halfback areas since the quarterback will shift to these positions often. The snaps should be soft, yet firm. Remind the center that he will not need the force in the snap that is required when making a long snap to a punter 12-13 yards deep. By all means, never use the *Quarterback Shift* plays until the center has become proficient in his short snaps.

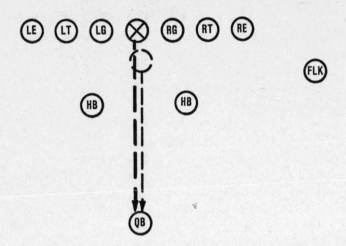

Figure 35-4 *Quarterback shifts to punt formation.*

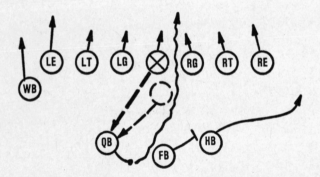

Figure 35-5 *Quarterback shifts to halfback position for a quick kick.*

Play 36

Quarterback in Motion

Why would a quarterback ever be sent in motion? This is a very logical question and has a simple answer. Quarterbacks are always among a team's best athletes. In most cases in high school, the quarterback *is* the team's best athlete. Your opponents know this. Therefore, when he starts in motion, the defense had better react to him. If the defense makes no adjustment, the quarterback can hurt them in several ways. If the defense does react to the quarterback's motion, it can create openings in the defense that the offensive team can take advantage of.

There are five ways to benefit from a quarterback in motion:

1. *The quarterback can be used as a pass receiver*. Of course, to use him as a receiver, another backfield member must be an adequate passer. The best time to use the quarterback in motion as a pass receiver is when the opposing team is using a man-to-man

defense, because seldom will the defense assign a player to cover the quarterback. Figure 36-1 shows the quarterback in motion to the right, with a flanker and a tight split backfield. The defense is in a 6-2 man-to-man defense and there is no one to take the quarterback. (*Note:* As with all plays in this section, the center must be able to make a short, soft snap to a halfback or fullback.)

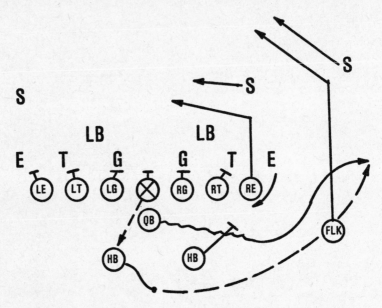

Figure 36-1 *Defense is 6-2 man-to-man with safety men covering the ends and flanker and inside linebackers covering the halfbacks. No one is assigned to cover the quarterback.*

2. *The quarterback can be used as a lead blocker.* Some coaches will prefer not to allow their quarterback to block for fear of injury, which of course is a possibility. However, we have never had one injured blocking and have gained good yardage as a result of the blocks of our quarterbacks. Figure 36-2 shows a power sweep by the fullback with the quarterback in motion as a lead blocker.

3. *The quarterback can be used as a decoy.* Since most good defensive teams will respect the motion of a good quarterback, his movement can be used to cause a defensive secondary rotation or to pull a linebacker out of his normal position. Figure 36-3 shows

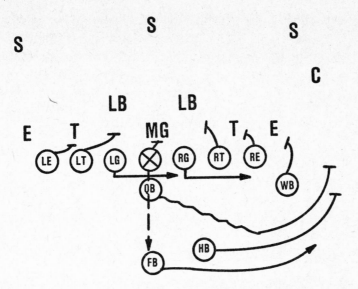

Figure 36-2 *Quarterback in motion leads fullback power sweep.*

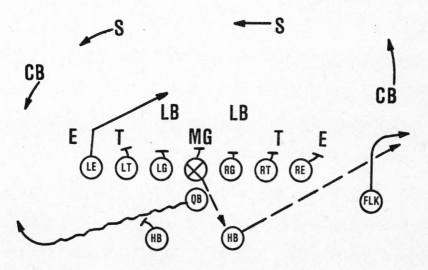

Figure 36-3

how the quarterback's motion causes a defensive backfield rotation which provides room for a quick turn-out pass to the flanker.

4. *The quarterback's motion will often cause a defensive*

player to jump offsides. You should understand that the quarterback can not make any sudden movement with the hands or other parts of his body in an effort to force an offsides by the defense. This is not legal or ethical. However, motion by the quarterback after he has approached the line of scrimmage and after being still for one second is legal. This movement, in itself, is sometimes enough to cause a defensive reaction across the line of scrimmage.

5. *The quarterback's motion can put him in good position to cover a quick kick.* Many quarterbacks have good speed. This speed is wasted if the quarterback's job on a quick kick is to take the snap and toss the football to a halfback or fullback, who then kicks it. By sending the quarterback in motion and having a direct snap from center to kicker, not only will you provide for a quicker kick, but you will provide speedy coverage by the quarterback (see Figure 36-4).

Since quarterbacks usually don't go in motion, you must teach your quarterback the fundamentals of going in motion, such as moving away from the line of scrimmage during motion and not turning upfield too soon. Remember, also, to plan to have a halfback or fullback call the snap count since the quarterback in motion won't be able to do it.

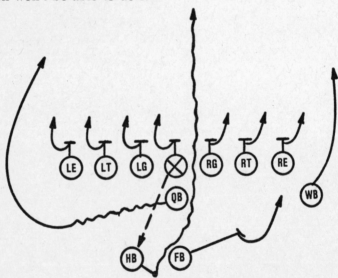

Figure 36-4 *Quarterback in motion covers quick kick.*

Play 37

Two Center Formation

The *Two Center Formation* is one of the most unusual surprise formations possible and can be extremely beneficial to any team that uses an unbalanced line or desires to use an unbalanced line occasionally.

The formation is set up in this way:

1. Remove the two guards from the lineup and replace them with two centers. This is not so difficult to do, as many teams have a capable second string, or back-up, center.

2. Place one offensive guard at the normal center position. When these two steps are completed, the offensive line will appear as shown in Figure 37-1.

Here's how to utilize the formation:

1. The offensive team breaks the huddle, and as the offensive linemen approach the line of scrimmage, they all assume a two-

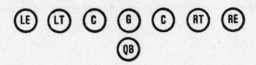

Figure 37-1 *Offensive line (with QB) before shift.*

point stance with their hands resting on their knees. Backfield personnel take their normal positions. The "guard" stands behind the football.

2. On command by the quarterback the entire offensive line will shift one position to the left or right depending on the play called in the huddle.

3. This shift will position one of the two centers over the football and will create an unbalanced line to the right or to the left (see Figures 37-2a & b).

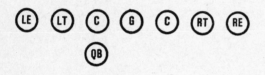

Figure 37-2a *Line shifts to right, creating unbalanced line to the right.*

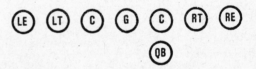

Figure 37-2b *Line shifts left, creating unbalanced line to the left.*

4. The players in the offensive backfield, by remaining in the positions they took as they broke the huddle, can cause further complications for the defense. For example, Figure 37-3 shows the offensive line before its shift, with the offensive backfield in a Power "I" formation to the offensive left side. If the offensive line shifts to the left the defense will be forced to make some adjustments or be outmanned on that side (see Figure 37-4).

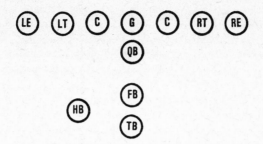

Figure 37-3 *Offensive line before shift with Power "I" backfield to the left side.*

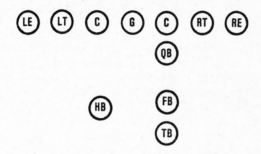

Figure 37-4 *Offensive line shifts to the left, concentrating power on the left side.*

If the offensive line shifts to the right we have an unbalanced line to the right (giving strength to that side) together with a strong backfield to the left side (see Figure 37-5).

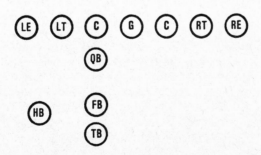

Figure 37-5 *Unbalanced line to the right side with backfield power to the left side.*

5. Backfield shifts can also take place along with the offensive line shifts, causing further problems to the defense. Each coach should experiment with his own offensive backfield formation to determine which, if any, backfield shifts would be helpful.

Coaching Points:

All offensive linemen must work to develop their shift so that they will be moving in unison. The linemen should step together and all take their three- or four-point stances at the same time. The quicker they all get set and remain still for one second, the sooner the football can be snapped. Never give the defense time to figure out what you are doing and allow them to make sound adjustments.

The quarterback must also remember that he will be working with two different centers. He may have to make an adjustment in his stance depending on the size of the centers (one center may be 6'3" and 190 lbs. and the other 5'9" and 155 lbs.). He must also keep in mind that one center will snap a little quicker than the other, or that one's snap may be softer than the other's. Be sure that both centers are capable snappers and that the quarterback has ample practice time with each one.

Play 38

Adjusting Line Splits

Most defensive players are coached to line up in relation to a particular offensive player. For example, a defensive player may be told to line up on the outside shoulder of the offensive tackle, or to stay head-up on the offensive end. Therefore, when an offensive lineman widens his line split, the defensive player over him will usually move with him. This creates a greater distance between the defensive lineman and his nearest teammate. This also provides an excellent hole for the runner to carry the football through (see Figure 38-1).

If an offensive lineman closes his line split (gets closer to the offensive lineman to his inside) the defensive player will probably move with him, providing more room to carry the football to the outside (see Figure 38-2). The proper use of line splits can be invaluable to an offensive team.

There are two points to remember when planning to use offensive line splits:

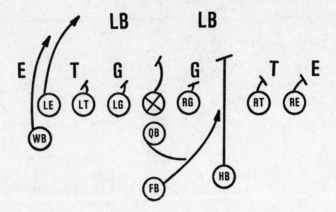

Figure 38-1   *Right tackle widens his split. Defensive tackle moves with him. A large hole is created for the ball carrier.*

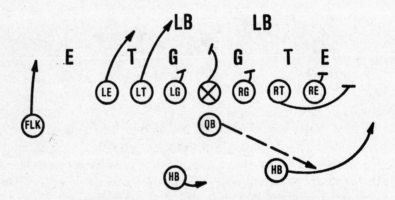

Figure 38-2   *Offensive linemen on the right side (RE, RT, and RG) have all closed their splits, bringing defensive players closer to the inside. This enables the ball carrier to get outside more quickly.*

1. Some teams will be poorly coached concerning how to react to offensive line splits. These teams can be manipulated easily and large holes can be created in the defensive line.

2. Most teams have been coached to some extent concerning handling line splits, but as the game progresses, defensive players

will be less likely to notice small line splits as they grow, play by play, into large line splits.

There are two ways to teach offensive linemen to use line splits. Some coaches prefer to teach all linemen the basic idea of line splits (get a large split if ball is coming inside of you and get a smaller split if ball is going outside of you) and then let each individual player be responsible for making the proper adjustment at the proper time. Other coaches like to have their line splits called in the huddle. *Example:* If an offensive play is being run into the "3" hole, the call in the huddle could be "Split 3, 53 Lead," meaning for the players at hole "3" to split, giving more running room for the ball carrier as he runs through the "3" hole.

There are two ways to show offensive line splits to the defense:

1. Show line splits gradually (a few inches each play) so they will generally go unnoticed.

2. Show unusually large line splits all at once so that they will cause confusion among defensive players. If a large line split is shown all at once, the defensive player will either not know how to react and will take an unusually large split himself, or he will ignore the large split, remain where he is without moving and give the offensive blocker a tremendous blocking angle (see Figures 38-3a & b).

One of the best areas of line splits is between an offensive end and an offensive tackle. Often known as a "nasty" end, this split has given many defensive teams trouble. Let's assume an offensive end normally gets a three-foot split from the tackle. With the "nasty" end split, the end is about six to seven feet from the tackle. Figures 38-4a, b & c show how this creates problems for a defensive end in a 5-4 defense. If the defensive end moves out with the offensive end and remains on his outside, a large hole develops off-tackle. If the defensive end does not move from his normal position the offensive end has a great blocking angle on him, and a play can be run outside. If the defensive end gets head-on the offensive end, he cannot play his normal technique and the offensive end should be able to block him by firing straight into him and driving the defensive end in any direction he chooses to go (with the ball carrier cutting off the block).

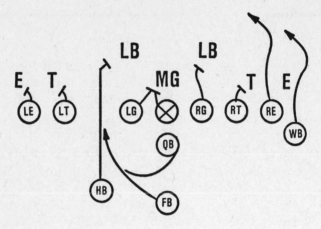

Figure 38-3a *The defensive tackle on the left side does not know how to react to a large line split and goes out with the left tackle. This opens a hole between the left guard and tackle.*

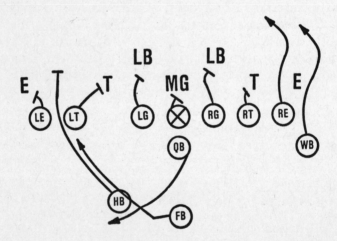

Figure 38-3b *The defensive tackle on the left side remains in his normal position and does not move out as the left tackle moves out. This gives the left tackle a great blocking angle for an off-tackle play.*

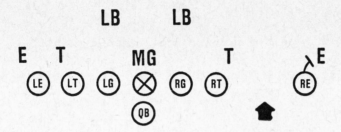

Figure 38-4a *Nasty End. The defensive end moves out with the nasty end, creating a large hole off tackle.*

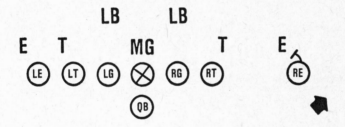

Figure 38-4b *The defensive end remains in normal position. The right end has a great blocking angle as the play is run outside.*

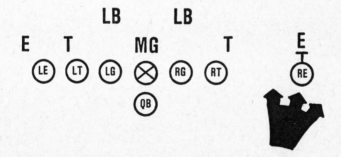

Figure 38-4c *The defensive end gets a head-on block. The nasty end blocks him straight ahead, taking him in whatever direction he can. The ball carrier cuts off the block.*

In summary, offensive linemen should be convinced of the importance of line splits, and daily drills should be used to effectively teach how to use line splits best for maximum offensive yardage.

Play 39

Triple Wide Formation

The *Triple Wide Formation* will force the defense into an unusual pass-defense coverage. The formation should only be used by a team that likes to pass and has a good passer along with several good receivers.

Figure 39-1 shows the basic *Triple Wide Formation*. The three wide receivers can be placed on the left side as well as on the right. One of the receivers will be an end. The other two will be backs. However, some coaches may prefer to use extra ends in place of the two receiving backs if good substitute ends are available who can catch better than the backs. Or, if a good substitute back is available, the coach may want to use him in place of the normal end (who might have been a starter because of his blocking ability rather than his pass catching ability). At any rate, get the team's three best receivers in the three wide receiver positions.

The third back (other than the quarterback) should be a good blocker, for he will be the only protection for the passer other than

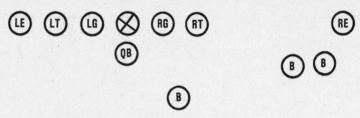

Figure 39-1 *Basic Triple Wide Formation*

the offensive linemen. This back will also be called on to carry the football and should be an adequate runner.

In defending against the *Triple Wide Formation*, it will be necessary for three secondary players to move into the area of the three receivers and, in most cases, cover them man-to-man.

When the formation is shown for the first time, the play will probably work because of confusion in the defensive secondary. At this point, the defensive coach will probably call time out and send in instructions concerning how to cover the receivers. After this is done, the offensive coach should begin looking for ways to create mismatches between the receivers and the secondary defenders. (*Note*: A good scouting report before the game will give the offensive coach knowledge as to the fastest defensive back, the slowest, the best jumper and so on.) It is then up to the offensive coach to arrange his receivers in position to cause a mismatch between the primary receiver and the player covering him. For example, the first time the formation is called the receivers and defenders may match up as shown in Figure 39-2. The offensive coach can rear-

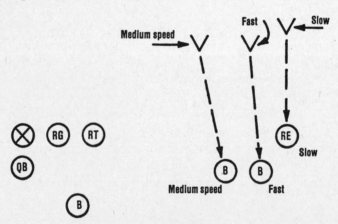

Figure 39-2

range his receivers so that the fastest receiver can be matched with the slowest defender as shown in Figure 39-3.

There are untold numbers of pass routes that can be worked out for the three receivers. Figure 39-4 shows one of the best routes. The end starts his release downfield but stops suddenly and returns to the line of scrimmage to catch a quick pass from the quarterback. With the defensive backs retreating quickly as all three receivers seem to be releasing from the line of scrimmage, it will be almost impossible for a defensive back to come up fast enough to stop the completion.

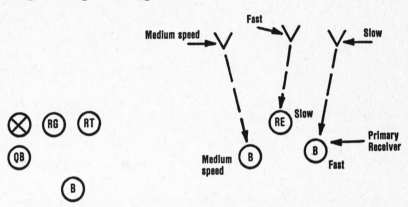

Figure 39-3

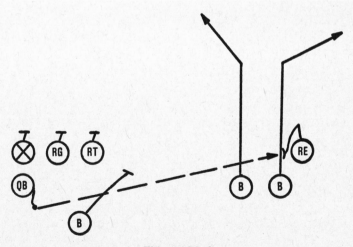

Figure 39-4

Figure 39-5 shows a crossing-type pass route that is very difficult to cover.

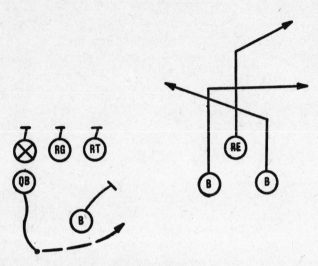

Figure 39-5

To keep the defense honest the "blocking" back should be given the football often on running plays. He can be placed at any running back position. Figure 39-6 illustrates how the back, when

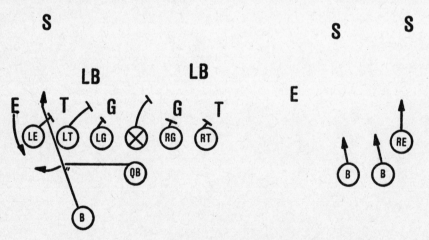

Figure 39-6   *Running play from Triple Wide Formation*

placed at left halfback, can run a veer-type play. Straight dive plays can be run from the fullback or either halfback position. Even an option play (see Figure 39-7) can be effective from the *Triple Wide Formation*.

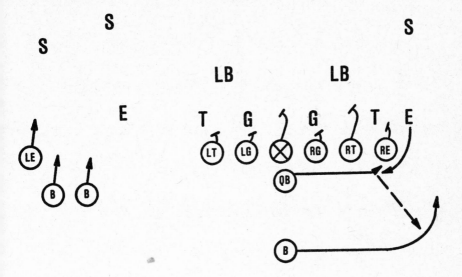

Figure 39-7 *Option play from Triple Wide Formation*

Play 40

Shifting Ends and Backs
to Confuse Man-to-Man
Pass Defense Assignments

The ideas connected with *Shifting Ends and Backs* are to be used only against teams that use a man-to-man pass defense. The goal of shifting ends and backs is to force the defensive secondary to have to wait until the very last moment to pick up the player each is to cover man-to-man. This can lead to much defensive confusion, and often two defensive backs will cover the same receiver while another eligible receiver goes unnoticed.

Two comments should be made before looking at how to use *Shifting Ends and Backs* to confuse man-to-man coverage. First, insist that all shifting ends and backs move quickly to their new positions and get set (down in stance) as soon as possible. The faster this is done, the less time the defensive secondary will have to determine which players are eligible and who will cover whom. Second, the diagrams shown here are drawn showing the offensive alignment as it will look to the defensive players (this is a slight change from other drawings in the book).

Start each play with the basic formation as shown in Figure 40-1. There are two split receivers (backs or ends). The tight end, upon breaking the huddle, takes a temporary position just behind the quarterback, about three yards off the line of scrimmage. On command of the quarterback, the tight end will shift to one of several offensive positions. The split receivers will either remain on the line of scrimmage or drop back one yard into the backfield. These movements, together with the shifting of the running backs, create a tough problem for secondary men as they try to determine who is eligible for a pass and who will cover each receiver.

Here are some examples of formations created by *Shifting Ends and Backs*. Notice that there will be from one to four eligible receivers on each side. The defensive secondary must determine who these people are and provide coverage for each one. And most important, they must make their decisions quickly.

(*Note*: In the following diagrams all eligible receivers are in darker circles.)

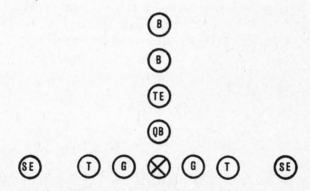

Figure 40-1 *Basic formation*

Figure 40-2 illustrates a formation with three eligible receivers (tight end, running back, and split receiver) on one side and two eligible receivers (split receiver and running back) on the other side. A split backfield offers good possibilities for a running play.

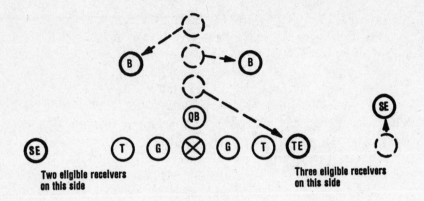

Two eligible receivers
on this side

Three eligible receivers
on this side

Figure 40-2

Figure 40-3 features a tight end, a split end, a flanker (split end moves into backfield), a slotback and one running back.

Figure 40-4 puts pressure on the defensive right side as four eligible receivers are on that side. Note that the tight end is actually in the backfield in this formation.

Figure 40-5 is a good running and passing formation. The split receivers have both moved in to tight end positions. The tight end is in a normal wingback position. A halfback and fullback complete the formation. Three eligible receivers are on one side, with one receiver on the other. The fullback can go either way.

In Figure 40-6 motion has been added after the shifts and can cause further problems for the defensive secondary. Motion to the

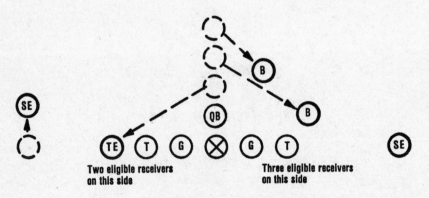

Two eligible receivers
on this side

Three eligible receivers
on this side

Figure 40-3

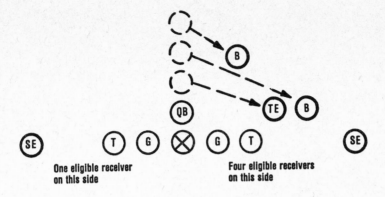

One eligible receiver
on this side

Four eligible receivers
on this side

Figure 40-4

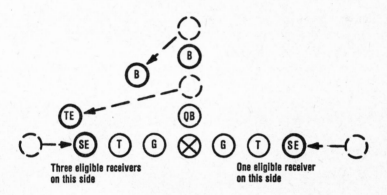

Three eligible receivers
on this side

One eligible receiver
on this side

Fullback can go either way

Figure 40-5

tight end's side will give three eligible receivers to the defensive right side. Motion to the side of the halfback will provide three eligible receivers to the defensive left side.

You are encouraged to experiment with your own players and find other formations created by shifting ends and backs. You should carefully watch the coverage on each formation so that you can best take advantage of defensive mistakes in man-to-man coverage.

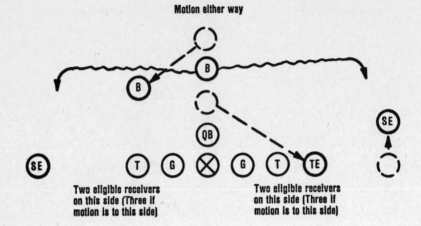

Figure 40-6

Play 41

Shifting Backfield Formations

The shifting of offensive backs from one position to another just before the ball is snapped is a movement used by many teams. It is very effective against any defense that overshifts its players toward what appears to be (before shifting the offensive backs) the strong side of the offense.

The shifting of backs is extremely easy to teach. Players enjoy the advantage they feel they are getting by shifting. If the shifting is done with planning and design it can definitely hurt the defensive effort.

Points for backs to remember are:

1. Break the huddle and get in position as if a play was ready to be run.

2. On the quarterback's command, shift quickly to your new position.

3. Take your stance and remain still for one second so that the ball can be snapped as rapidly as possible.

4. In some cases, you might have to be familiar with the assignments of several positions (since you will be shifting from one position to another). We feel that this is no problem and any back should have a good idea of how a play works at any backfield position.

Any type of backfield shift which will match offensive strength with defensive weakness should be used. Here are some examples of how to utilize shifting backs:

Figure 41-1a shows the offensive team in a Wing-T formation with the wingback on the right side. The defense has moved its defensive strength to that side. Suddenly, the wingback and halfback shift positions forming a Wing-T formation to the left side (Figure 41-1b).

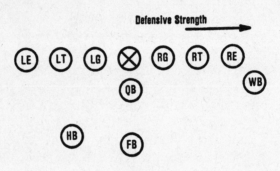

Figure 41-1a

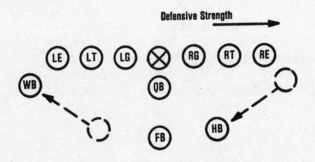

Figure 41-1b

Figure 41-2a illustrates a Power "I" formation with offensive strength to the left side, By shifting the tailback to right halfback and the left halfback to tailback the offensive power is now located on the right side (Figure 41-2b).

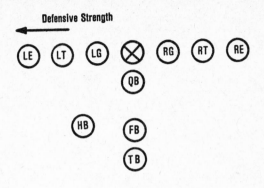

Figure 41-2a

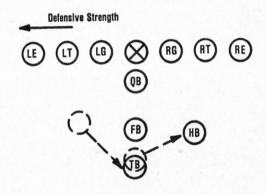

Figure 41-2b

Figures 41-3a & b change a formation featuring a wingback and an "I" backfield to a Power "I" formation on the left side.

Figures 41-4a & b start with an overloaded or "flood" set to the left and shift to a wingback (right side) and a split backfield formation.

A slot formation (Figures 41-5a & b) can quickly become a wing left "I" formation with the left halfback and slotback moving to new positions.

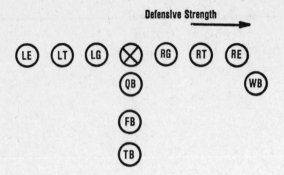

Figure 41-3a

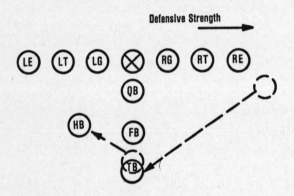

Figure 41-3b

Figure 41-4a

These are only a few of the many shift combinations that can be used. Each one will cause hesitation and uncertainty on the part of defensive players.

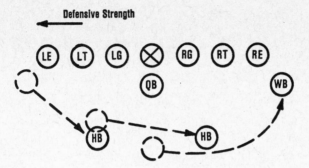

Figure 41-4b

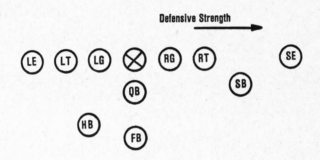

Figure 41-5a

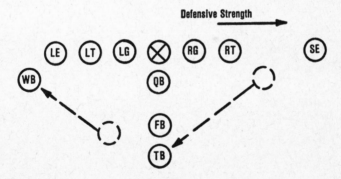

Figure 41-5b

Play 42

The Uneven "I"
Formation

The first time we used *The Uneven "I" Formation* it helped us beat an opponent who was a better team than we were and kept our playoff hopes alive. Our opponent was totally confused about how to defend it. We were not talented enough to overwhelm our opposition, but the *Uneven "I" Formation* kept the first downs coming when we needed them and gave us two scores in a 13-8 victory.

It features a line split between a guard and tackle on one side with an "I" alignment by two backs in the guard-tackle gap. There is a halfback on the other side of the formation. Figure 42-1 shows the *Uneven "I."*

There is no way a team can play a normal defense against this formation because adjustments must be made. When adjustments have been made, some defensive players find they are playing in different areas (*Example*: In a gap, rather than on an offensive

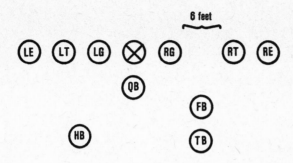

Figure 42-1 *The Uneven "I"*

player's outside shoulder) and using different techniques from those they had been taught before seeing the formation.

All types of plays—sweeps, traps, dives, crossbucks, options—can be run from the formation. You should choose plays that will take the best advantage of whatever adjustments the defense makes.

It is a good idea to make a lead (or isolation) play the first choice when selecting an opening play from the *Uneven "I" Formation* (see Figure 42-2). The lead play is a good choice, because if the

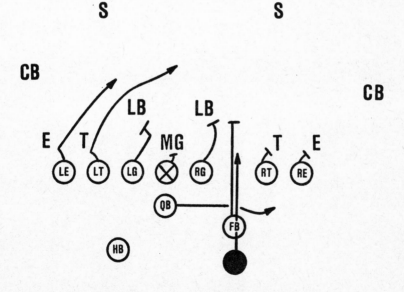

Figure 42-2 *Lead play from Uneven "I"*

defense doesn't adjust at all (the 5-4 defense in Figure 42-2 is drawn as it would appear if it didn't adjust), the hole will be wide open. The offense should continue running this lead play until the defense makes an adjustment to stop it. When they do make an adjustment that stops the lead play, some other area of defense will be weakened. Find this area and run a play directly at it.

Figure 42-3 shows how a 5-4 defense may try to adjust to the *Uneven "I"* and how a sweep play around the end can take advantage of their adjustment. (*Note*: We are not sure how any team will adjust so these diagrams are only our assumptions of how they *may* adjust.)

Figure 42-4 shows how most ordinary plays such as a crossbuck can be run from the *Uneven "I" Formation.*

Trap plays are also good, and the "front back" in the "I" formation is in perfect position to be a trap blocker (see Figure 42-5).

The list of plays possible from the *Uneven "I"* is a long one. Counters, quick pitches and almost anything can be run from the formation. Be sure to add passes (long, short and screen) plus

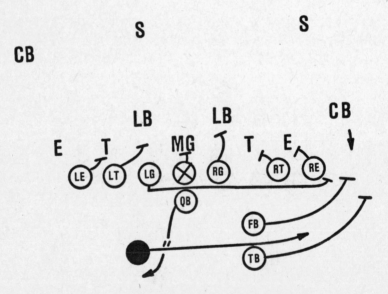

Figure 42-3 *Sweep from Uneven "I"*

send a back in motion occasionally, and the *Uneven "I"* will provide the offense with a surprise formation that is difficult to handle.

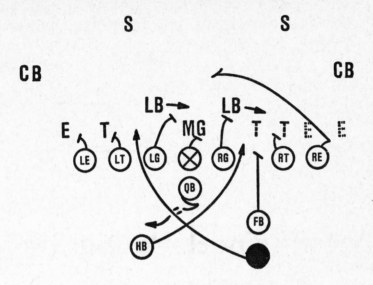

Figure 42-4 *Crossbuck from Uneven "I"*

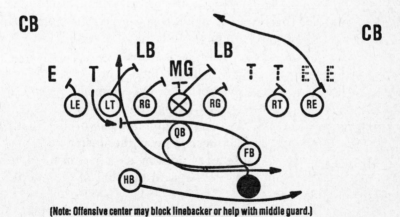

(Note: Offensive center may block linebacker or help with middle guard.)

Figure 42-5 *Trap from Uneven "I"*

Play 43

Quarterback-Halfback
Shift

This simple shift is designed to take advantage of all the talents that a quarterback and a halfback possess. The *Quarterback-Halfback Shift* should not be used too often, but it can be an excellent change from the normal offensive pattern.

The quarterback and halfback should break the huddle and take their normal offensive positions. On command by the quarterback, the two players quickly change positions (see Figure 43-1). After remaining still for one complete second, the football is snapped to the halfback who is now at the quarterback position. This shift will often cause an offsides by members of the defensive unit as they will not be familiar with the shift of the quarterback away from center.

Keep this key point in mind when relating to this play: Many halfbacks also have the ability to be good quarterbacks. By the same token, many quarterbacks are talented enough to be

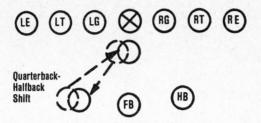

Figure 43-1

halfbacks. The quarterback-halfback shift gives both players the opportunity to use their talents at more than one position.

There are two good reasons for shifting a halfback to the quarterback position at some point in the game:

1. The halfback (now at quarterback) can use his speed to run a certain play such as a "quarterback bootleg" as shown in Figure 43-2.

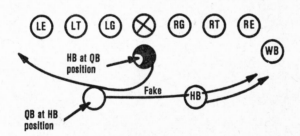

Figure 43-2

2. The halfback (now at quarterback) may be a more accurate long or short passer.

There are five good reasons for shifting the quarterback to halfback at some point in the game:

1. The quarterback (now at halfback), if he has excellent speed, can be used to run end sweep plays.

2. The quarterback (now at halfback) can be used to throw a *Fake End Sweep, Pass* play such as the one in Figure 43-3.

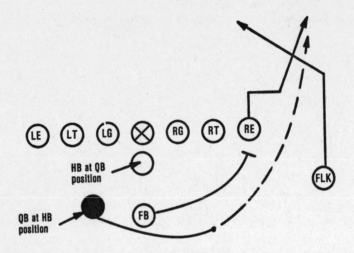

Figure 43-3

3. The quarterback (now at halfback) will be in position to handle the football on a reverse play where good ball handling by the "halfback" is necessary (see Figure 43-4).

4. The quarterback (now at halfback), because of his athletic ability, may be a good punter and could be used at the halfback position to quick kick the football (see Figure 43-5).

5. The quarterback (now at halfback) will be in position to be used as a blocker. *Example:* The quarterback may be 6'2", 195 lbs. By shifting him to halfback he would be a more effective blocker

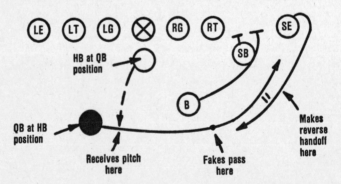

Figure 43-4   *Good ball handling by "quarterback" needed for this play.*

than the 5'8", 152 lb. regular halfback, who would have no assignment other than handing the football to a running back (see example in Figure 43-6).

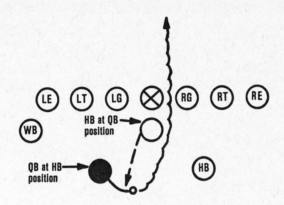

Figure 43-5

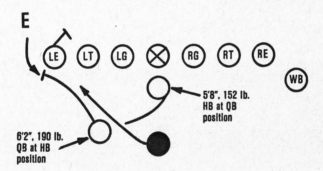

Figure 43-6

Play 44

End in Motion

To use the surprise movement of the *End in Motion* the offensive line must start with eight men on the line of scrimmage. This will leave three backfield men, but the end in motion will become the fourth back.

There are two ways to position the end in motion on the offensive line. In Figure 44-1 the end is the third lineman to the left of the center (same pattern can be used to the right side). As he goes in motion, the offensive team has an unbalanced line strong to the right side (four linemen on the right side of the football). This can create a good power attack to the strong side.

If the end is positioned as the fourth offensive lineman to the left of the football, a balanced line (three linemen on each side of the football) will remain once the end has started in motion (see Figure 44-2).

There must be a verbal command to send the end in motion since the end will not be in position to see the quarterback give a visual signal such as lifting his heel. The end must be taught all correct procedures for going in motion as this will be a new experience for him.

The *End in Motion* can be useful in four important ways:

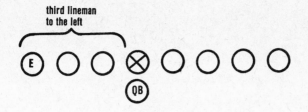

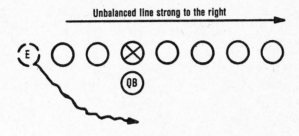

Figure 44-1

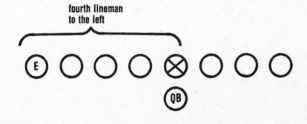

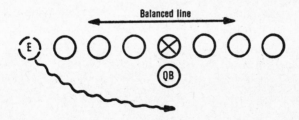

Figure 44-2

1. *He can be used as a blocker.* Figure 44-3 illustrates how the end in motion can be a lead blocker in a power sweep play toward the strong side of an unbalanced line.

Figure 44-3

2. *He can be used as a pass receiver.* Figure 44-4 shows a sample pass route featuring the end in motion running a little swing route to the outside. In Figure 44-5 the end is going in motion to his left (away from the offense). As the football is snapped the end is actually in the same position that a normal flanker (wide receiver) would be in most offensive sets.

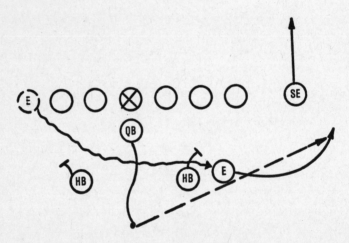

Figure 44-4

3. *The end in motion can be used as a ball carrier.* Figure 44-6 illustrates a power play off tackle with the end in motion carrying the football.

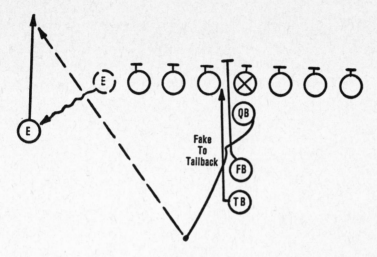

Figure 44-5

4. *The end in motion can be used as a decoy.* Especially if he has been effective as a pass receiver, his motion can cause a defensive rotation by the secondary which can open up a passing or running lane elsewhere (see Figure 44-7).

Remember that either end can be used in the *End in Motion* plays, doubling the problems for the defense.

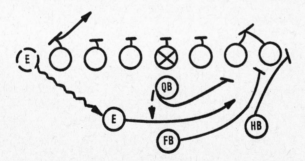

Figure 44-6

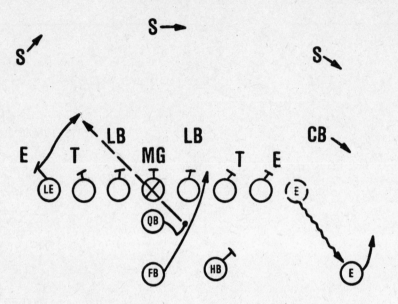

Figure 44-7 *Because of the end in motion, the secondary has rotated, opening a passing area for the left end.*

Play 45

Inside Slot Formation

There are two major differences between the *Inside Slot Formation* and the *Uneven "I" Formation* as described in Play 42:

1. The player who fills the inside slotback position is used almost entirely as a blocker and is lined up closer to the line of scrimmage than the similarly positioned player in the *Uneven "I" Formation*.

2. Unlike the *Uneven "I" Formation*, the other two running backs can be placed at any positions (such as fullback, either halfback, "I" formation behind the quarterback or wingback).

To set up this formation place the offensive linemen in their normal positions, but leave an extra four-foot split between the guard and tackle on one side. (*Note*: The *Inside Slot Formation* can be set to either side.) Insert a back in the slot between the guard and tackle making sure he is one yard off the line of scrimmage. Figure 45-1 shows the basic *Inside Slot Formation* (a fullback-left halfback combination is shown, but any backfield alignment can be used).

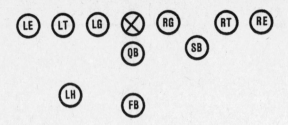

Figure 45-1 *Inside Slot Formation*

We believe strongly in this formation and like to use it late in the season as a change-up to our normal formations. It has never failed to cause the defense to be disorganized until their coach has made some adjustments. And most adjustments we have seen fail to completely stop the formation from being effective.

It is a very good idea to start the *Inside Slot Formation* to one side and continue it to the same side until the defense makes adequate adjustments (if it ever does). If defensive adjustments are successful in temporarily stopping the offense, just move the *Inside Slot Formation* to the other side of the line. It will now take the other side of the defensive line a while to make adjustments to the new formation, and by now the entire defense may be totally confused as to where to line up. All their week's work against normal offensive sets in practice will prove of little value against ·the *Inside Slot*.

As the *Inside Slot* alignment approaches the line of scrimmage, the defensive players will react in one of two ways. Either they will ignore it, line up on the same offensive man as usual and create a huge gap between guard and tackle, or they will attempt to adjust with each player adjusting in his own way. If the defense doesn't adjust, the gap will appear as shown in Figure 45-2. If the defense does adjust in some way, a defensive weakness will appear somewhere else.

Until adjustments are made on defense, all plays should be run into the guard-tackle-slotback area. As long as ground can be gained, keep hitting the same hole. The play shown in Figure 45-3 allows the slotback to block the linebacker with the right guard or to help the tackle with his man if help is most needed there.

A good power play off-tackle (Figure 45-4) can be run from the *Inside Slot Formation*. However, it is most important to remember

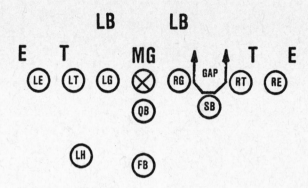

Figure 45-2 *The gap created in the 5-4 Defense due to the Inside Slot alignment.*

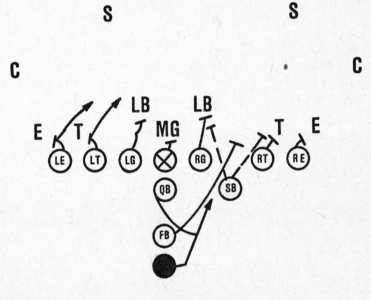

Figure 45-3

that if the *Inside Slot Formation* is used, plays should be run toward the inside slot area, as this is the defensive area this formation intends to make vulnerable.

Figure 45-5 shows a good crossbuck play into the inside slot area.

After convincing the defensive players that the inside slot area

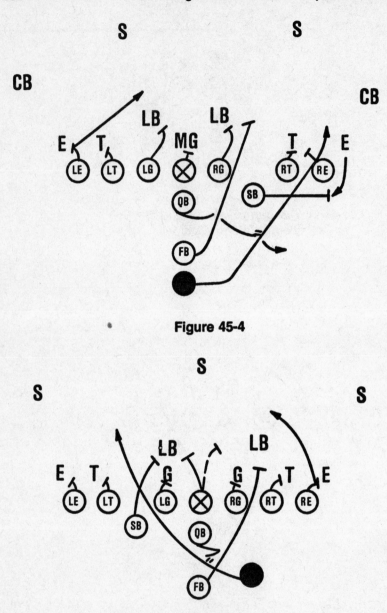

Figure 45-4

Figure 45-5

is the sole offensive target, plays such as the pass in Figure 45-6 can spring the inside slot "blocking back" loose in the defensive secondary.

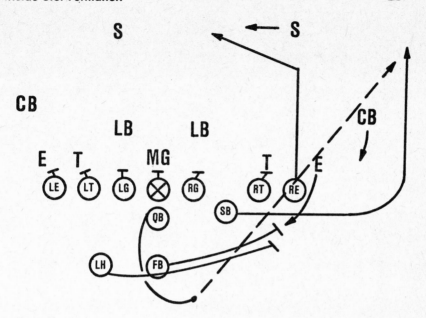

Figure 45-6

Index